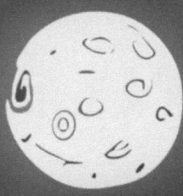

# ChromaVibes

## *COLORING BOOK*

Color Your Emotions, Write Your Thoughts

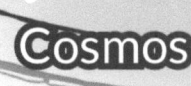

Cosmos

In the cosmos, we find the answers to questions we never knew to ask.

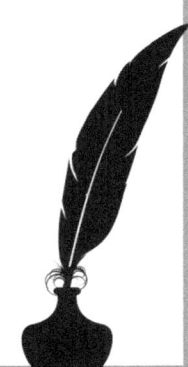

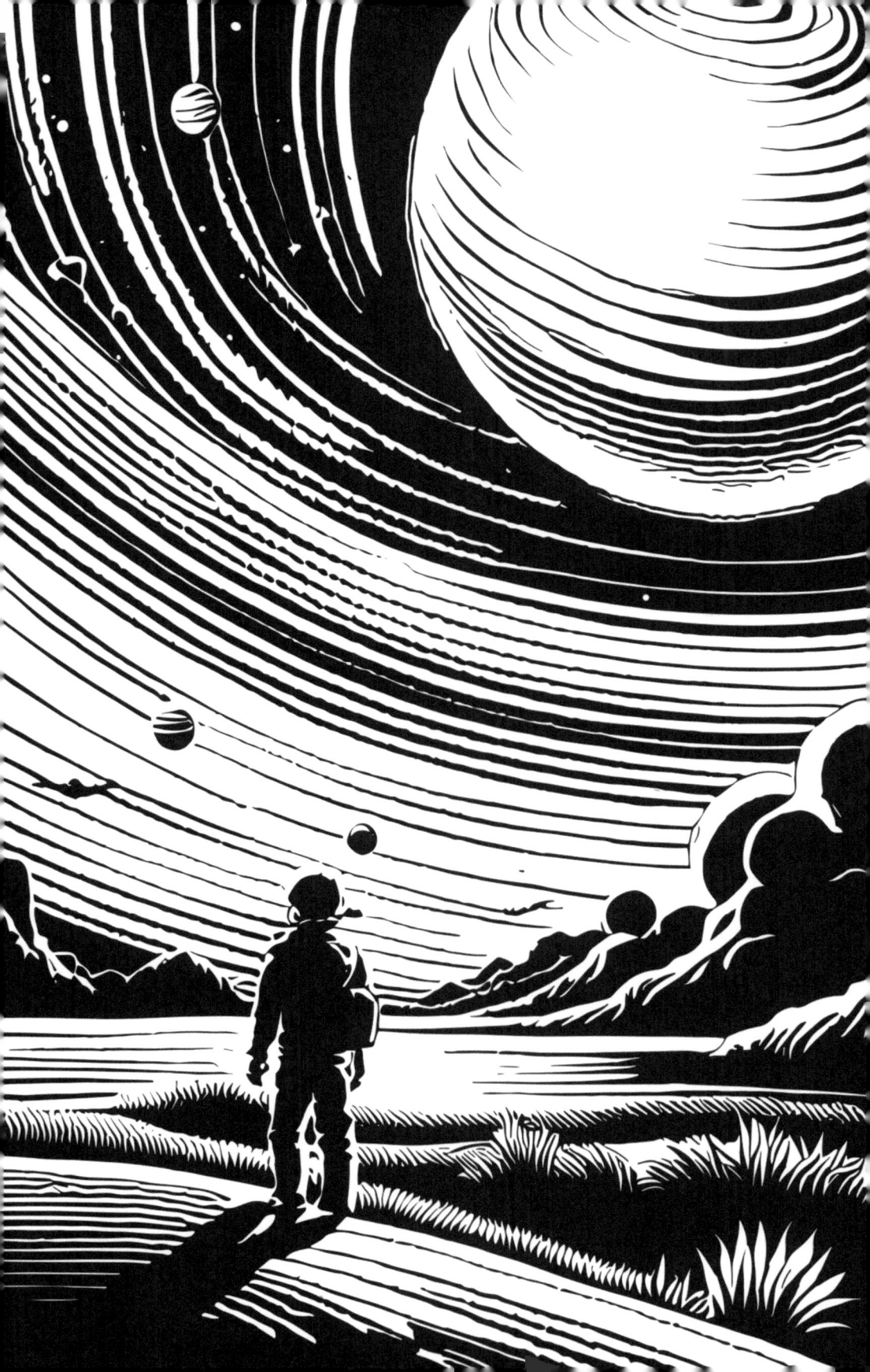

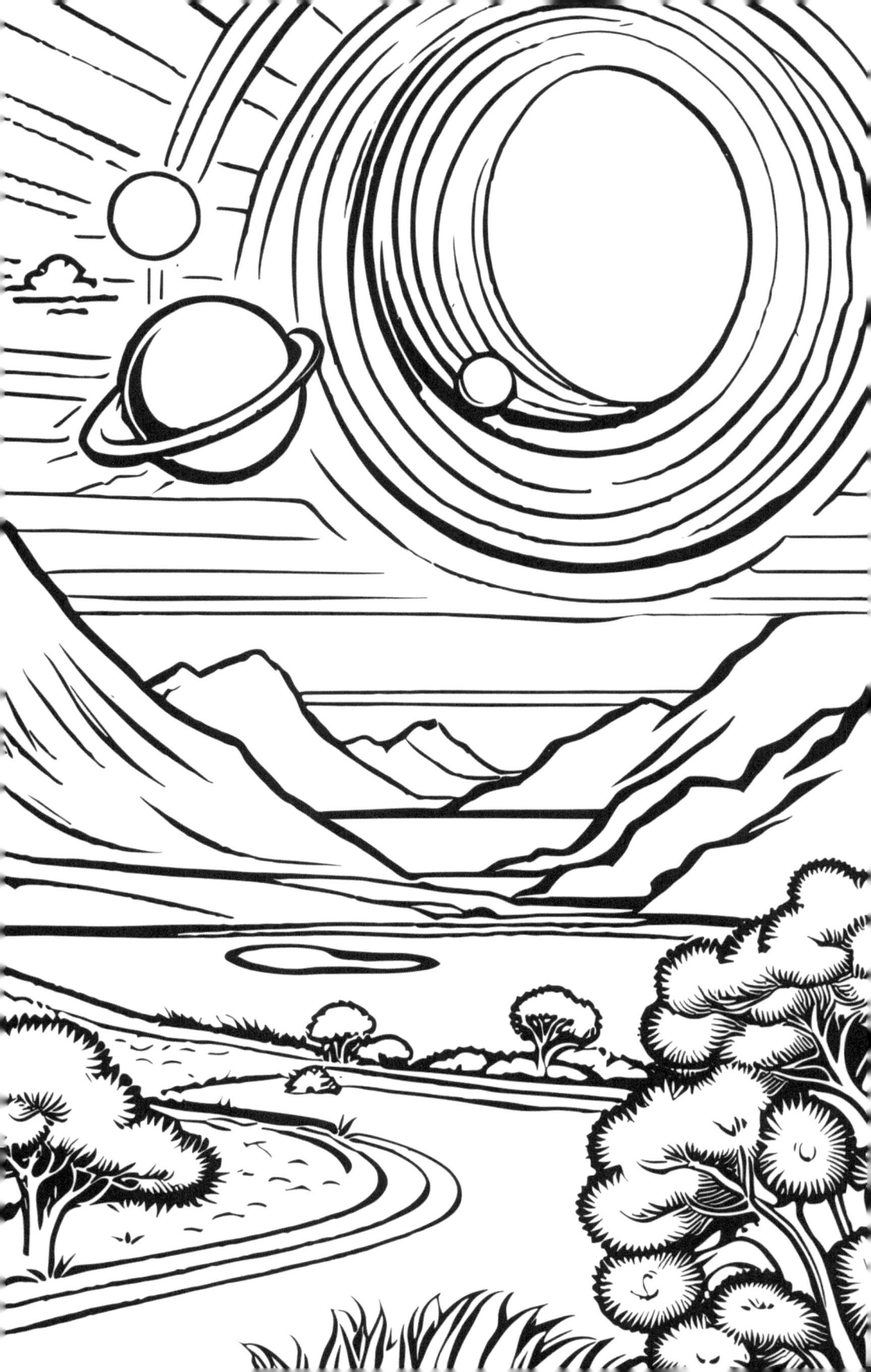

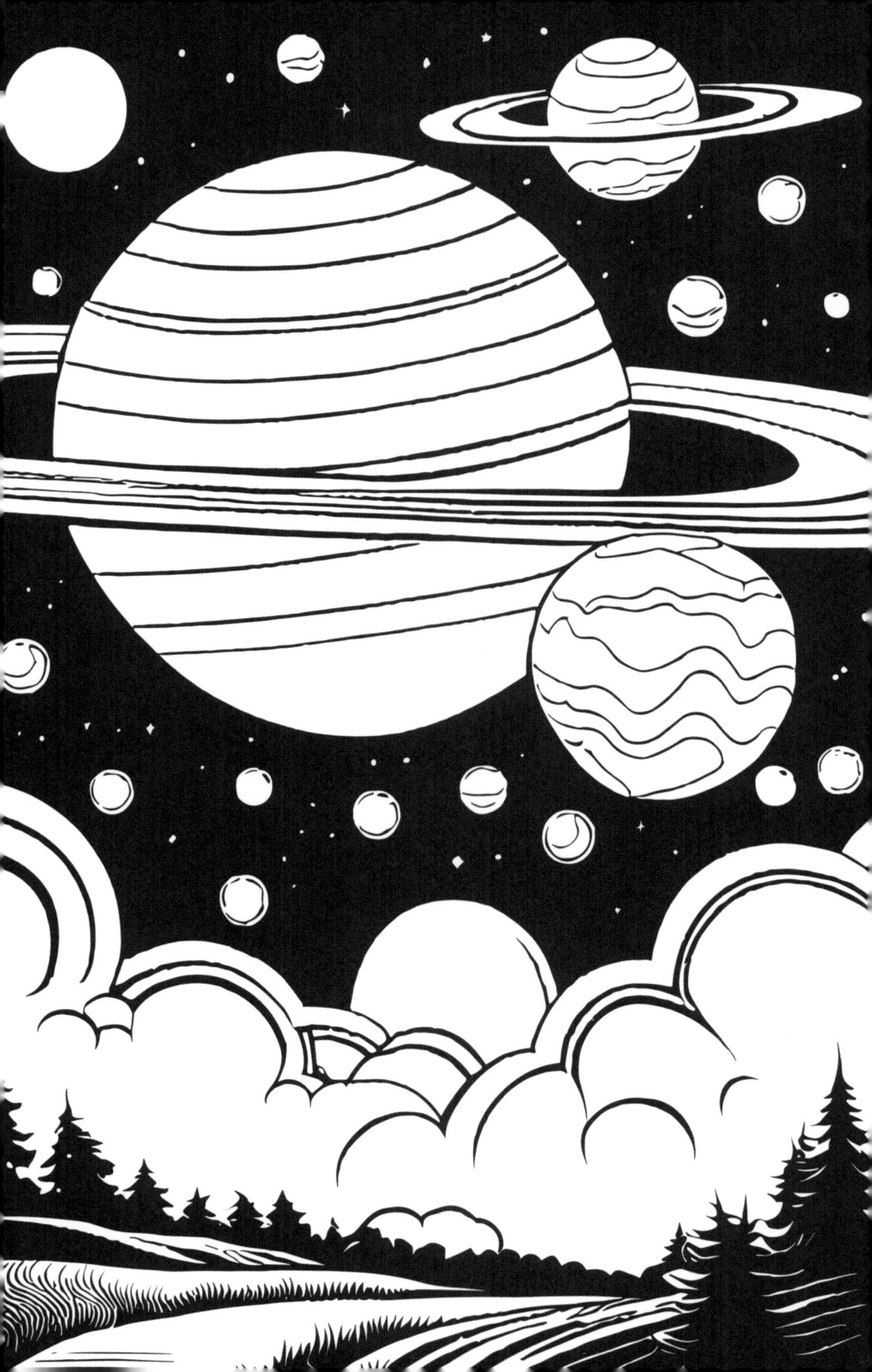

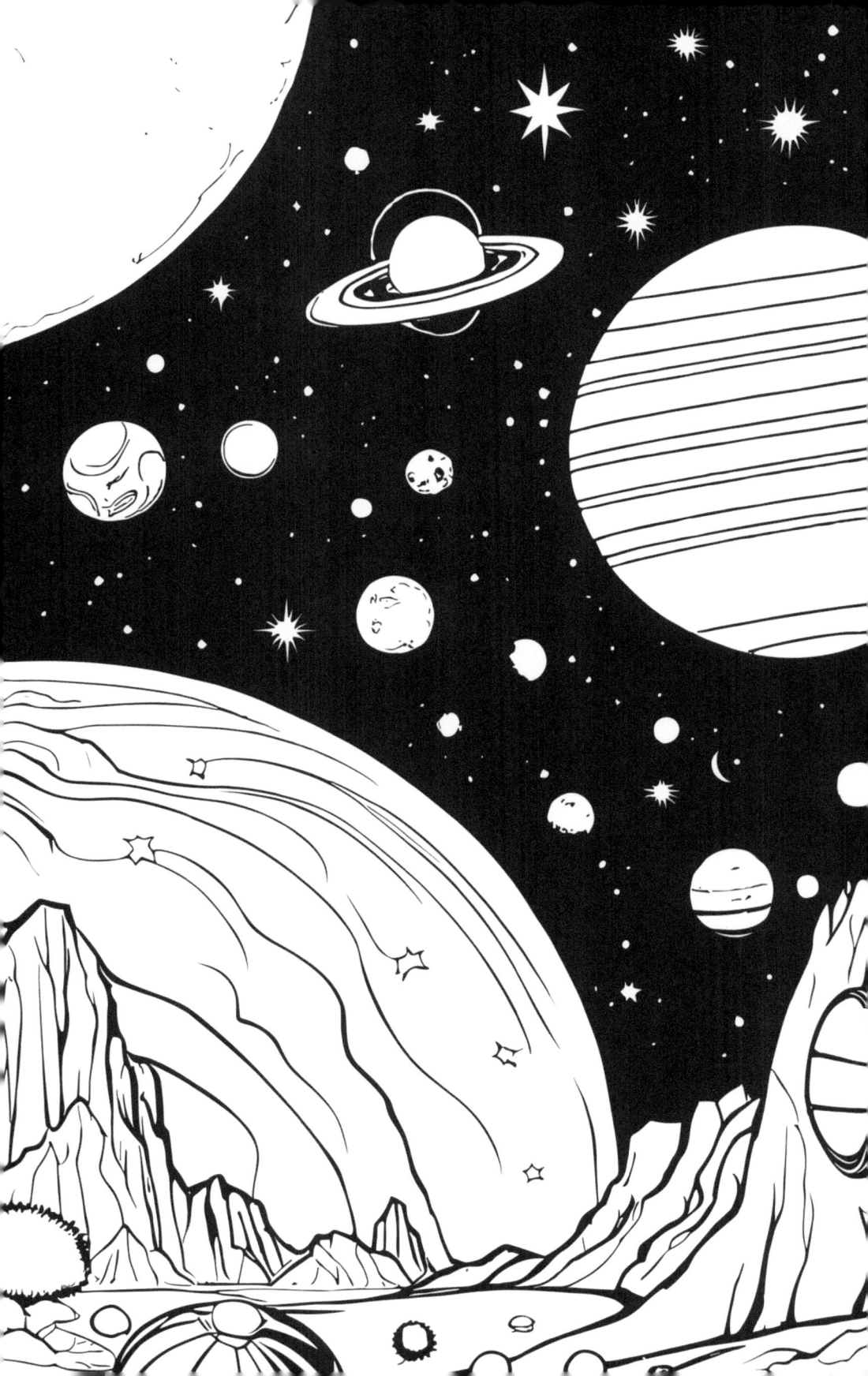

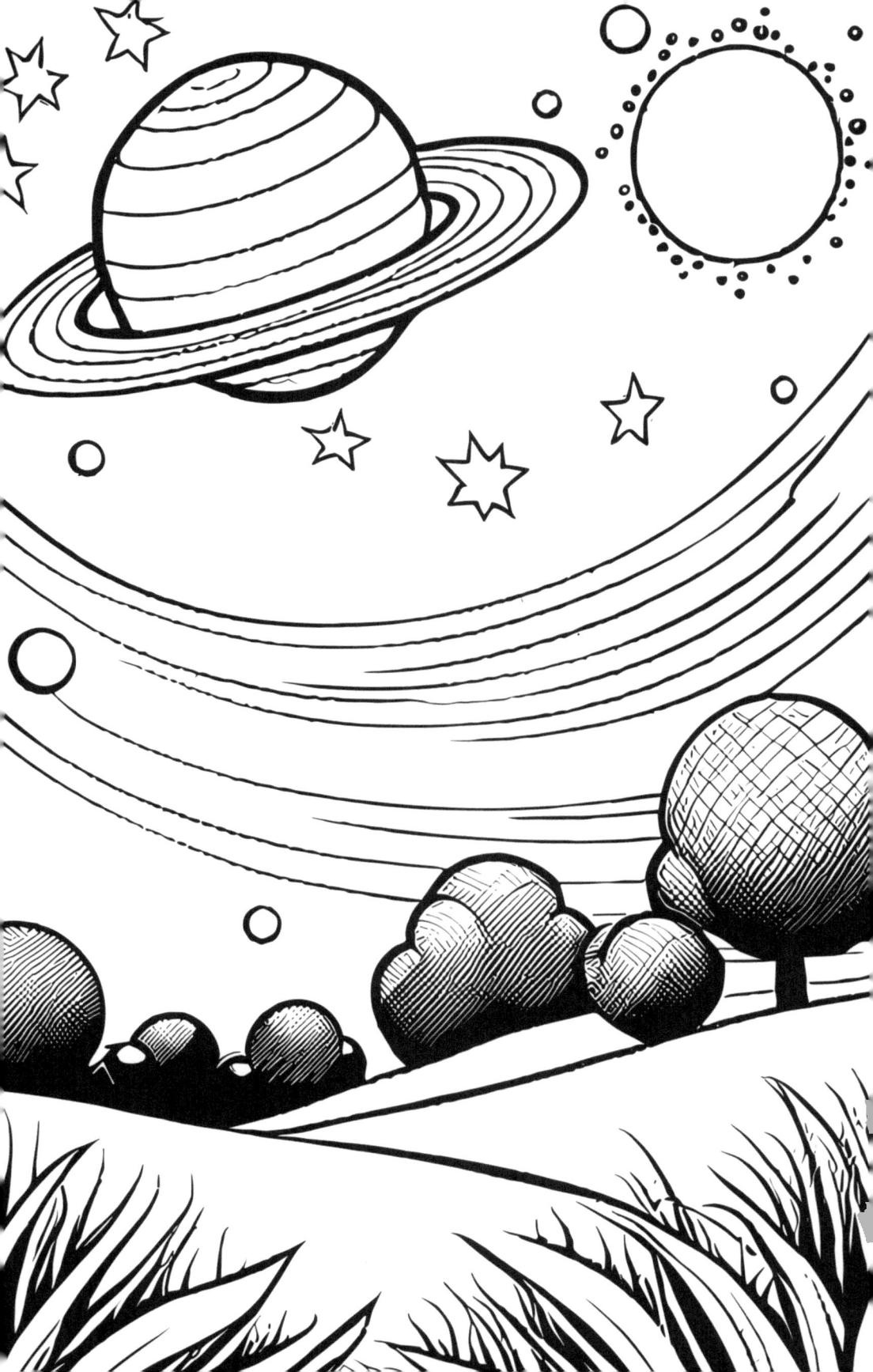

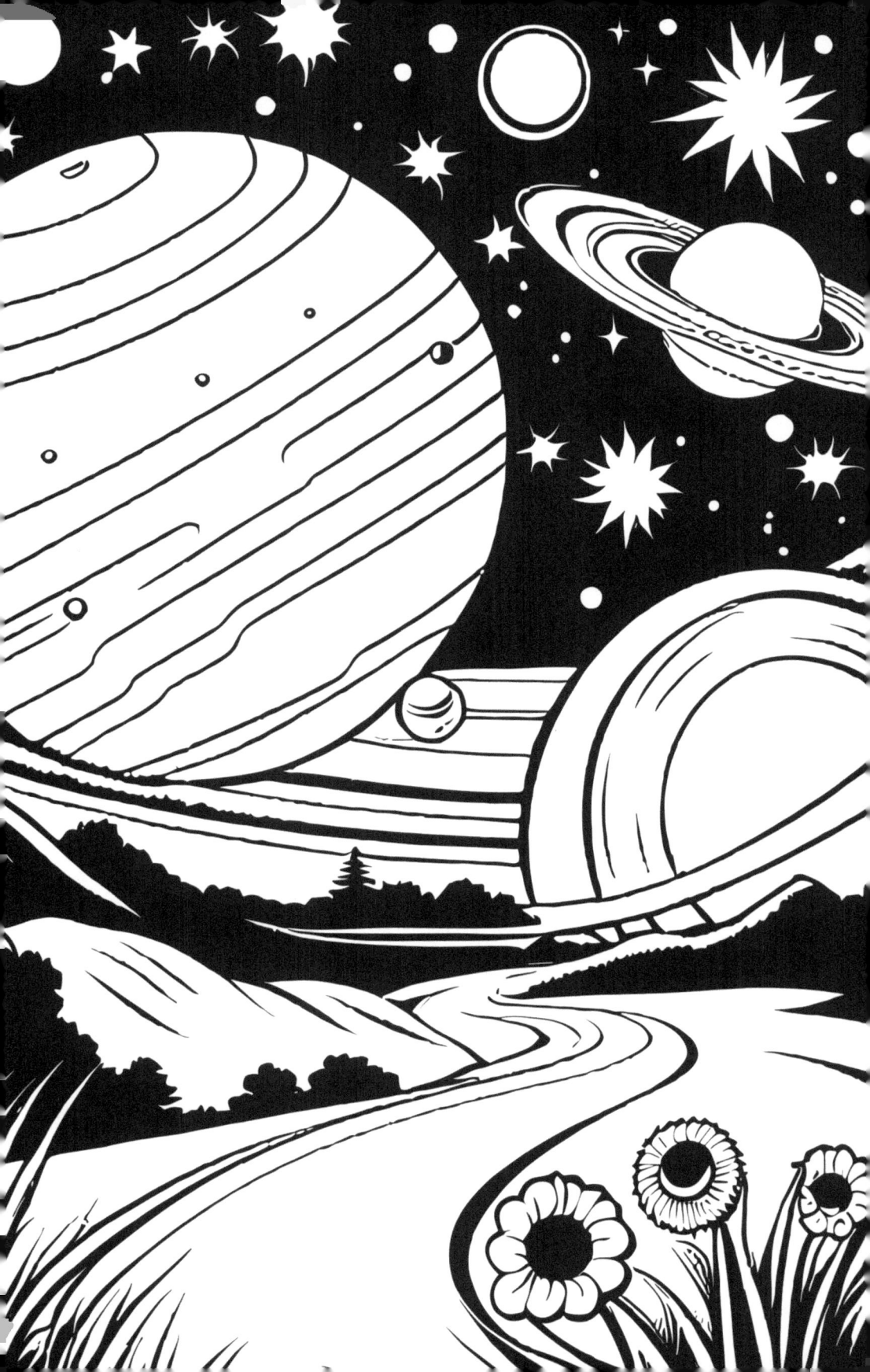

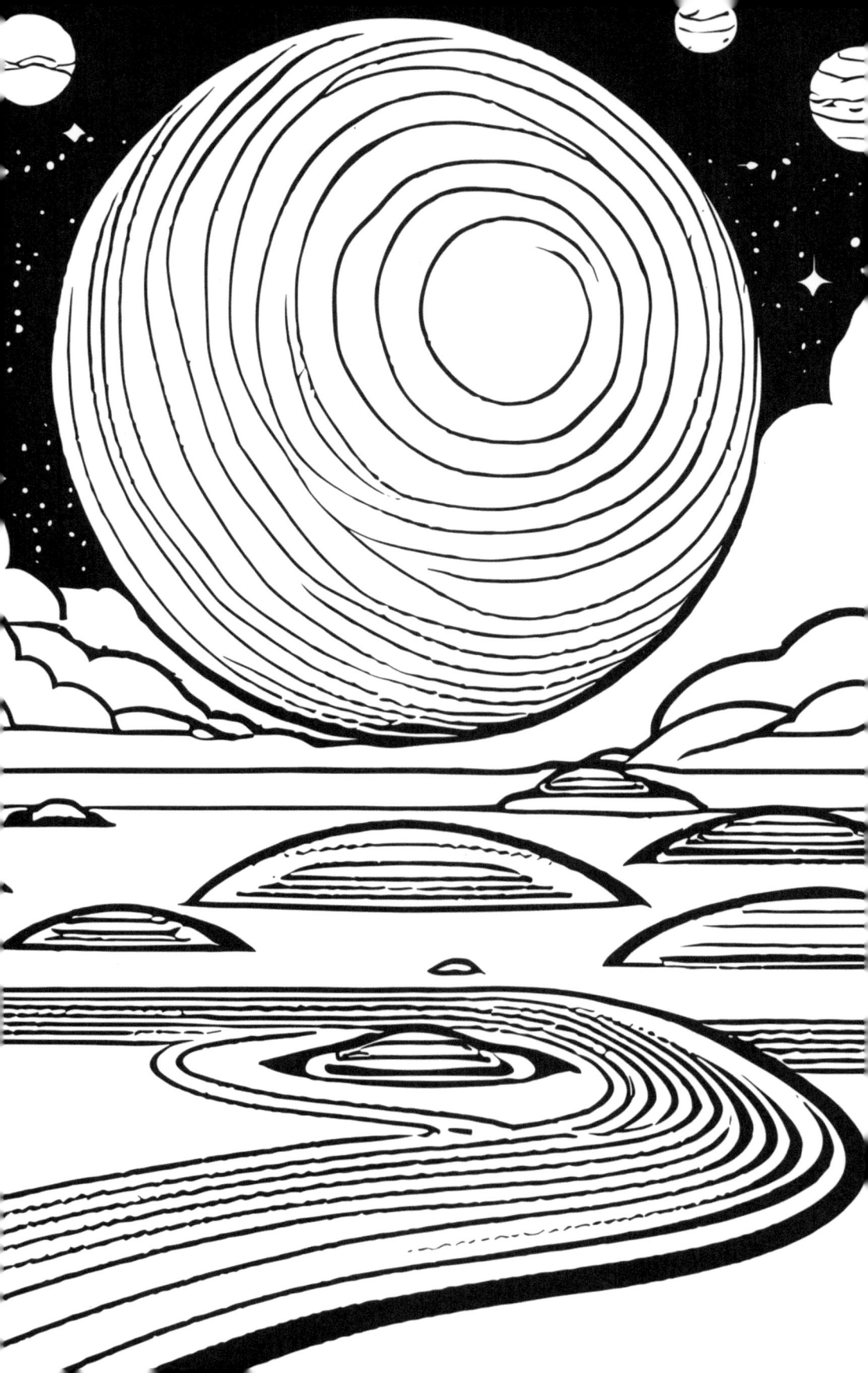

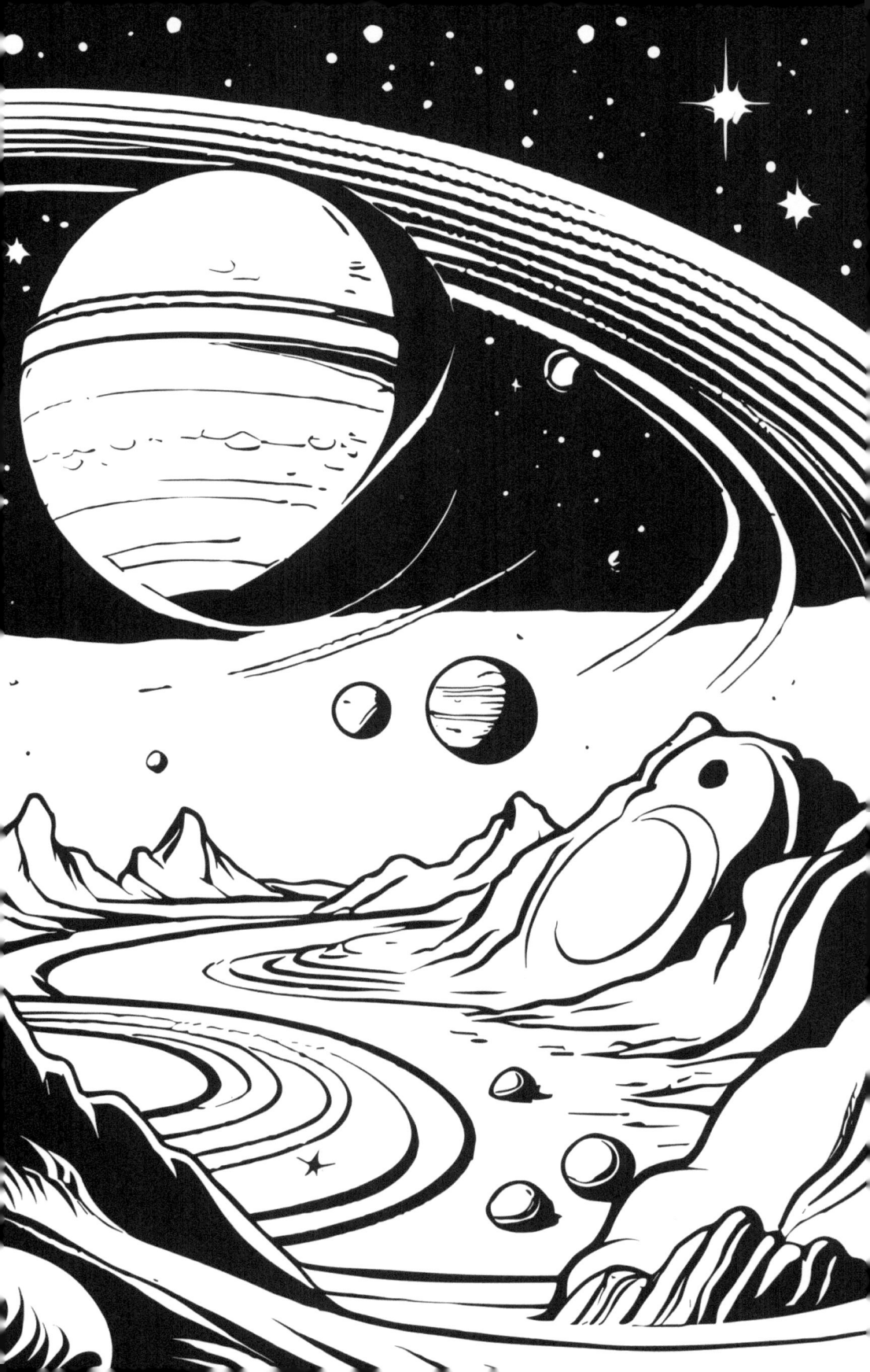

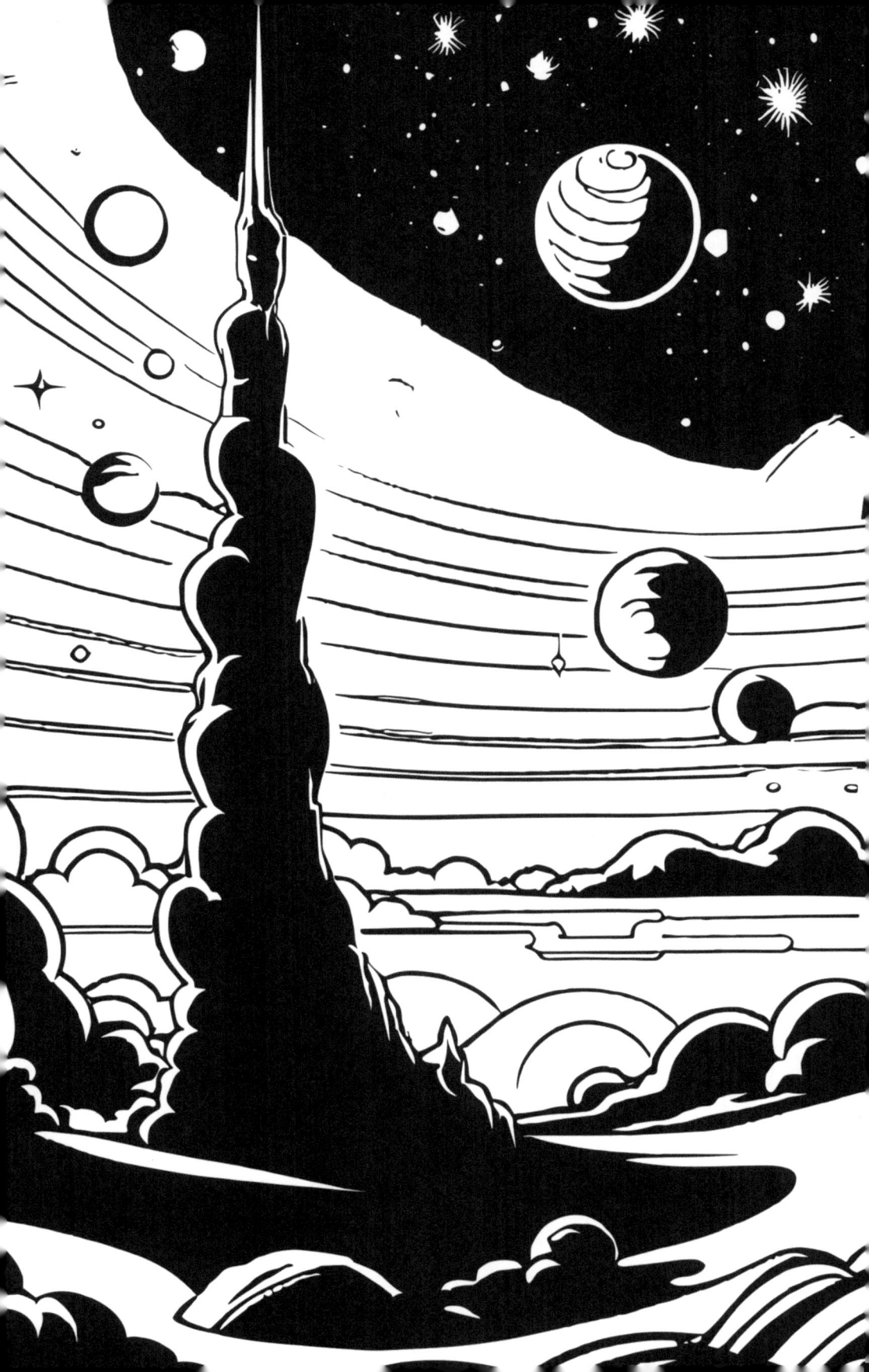

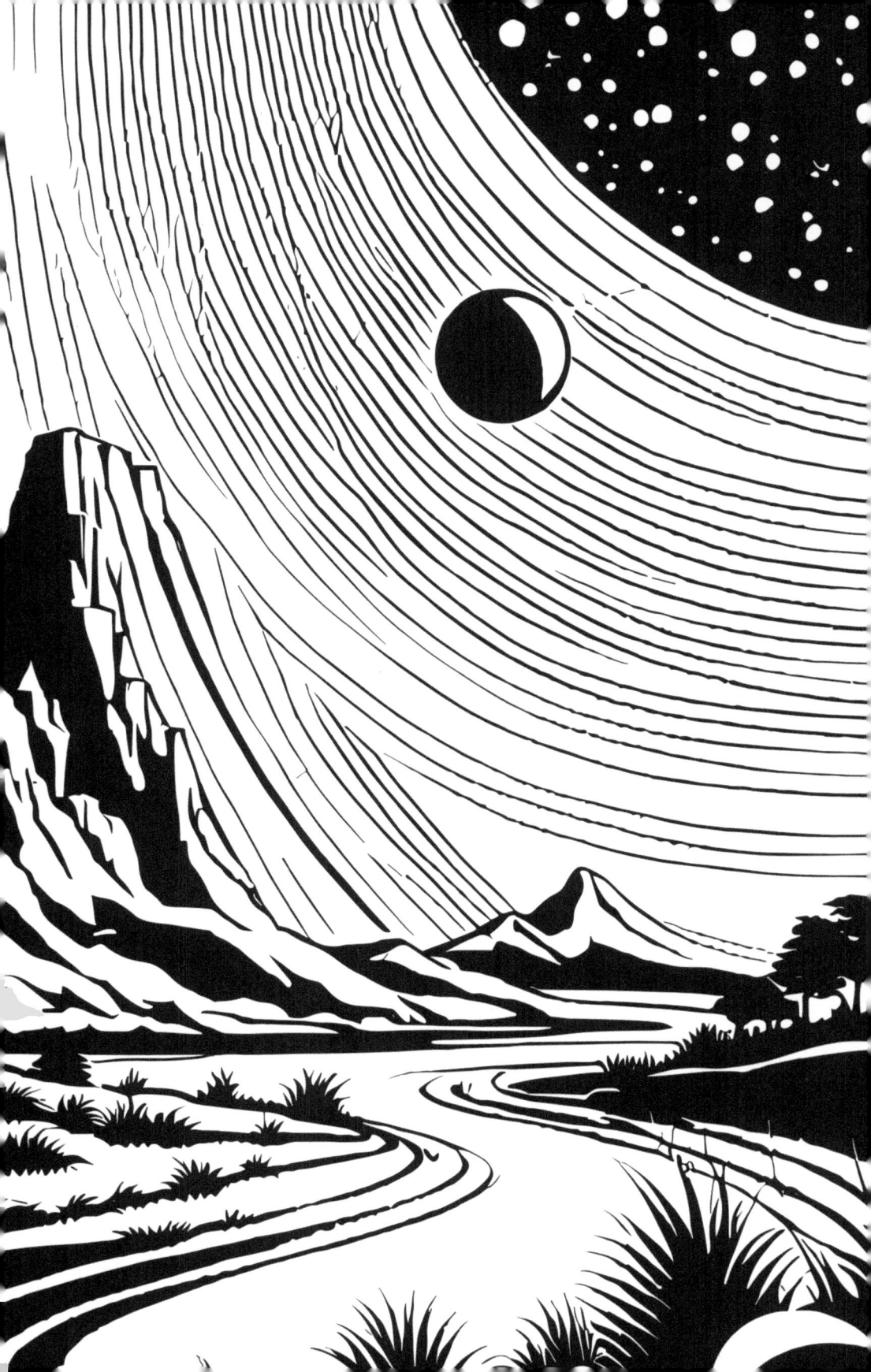

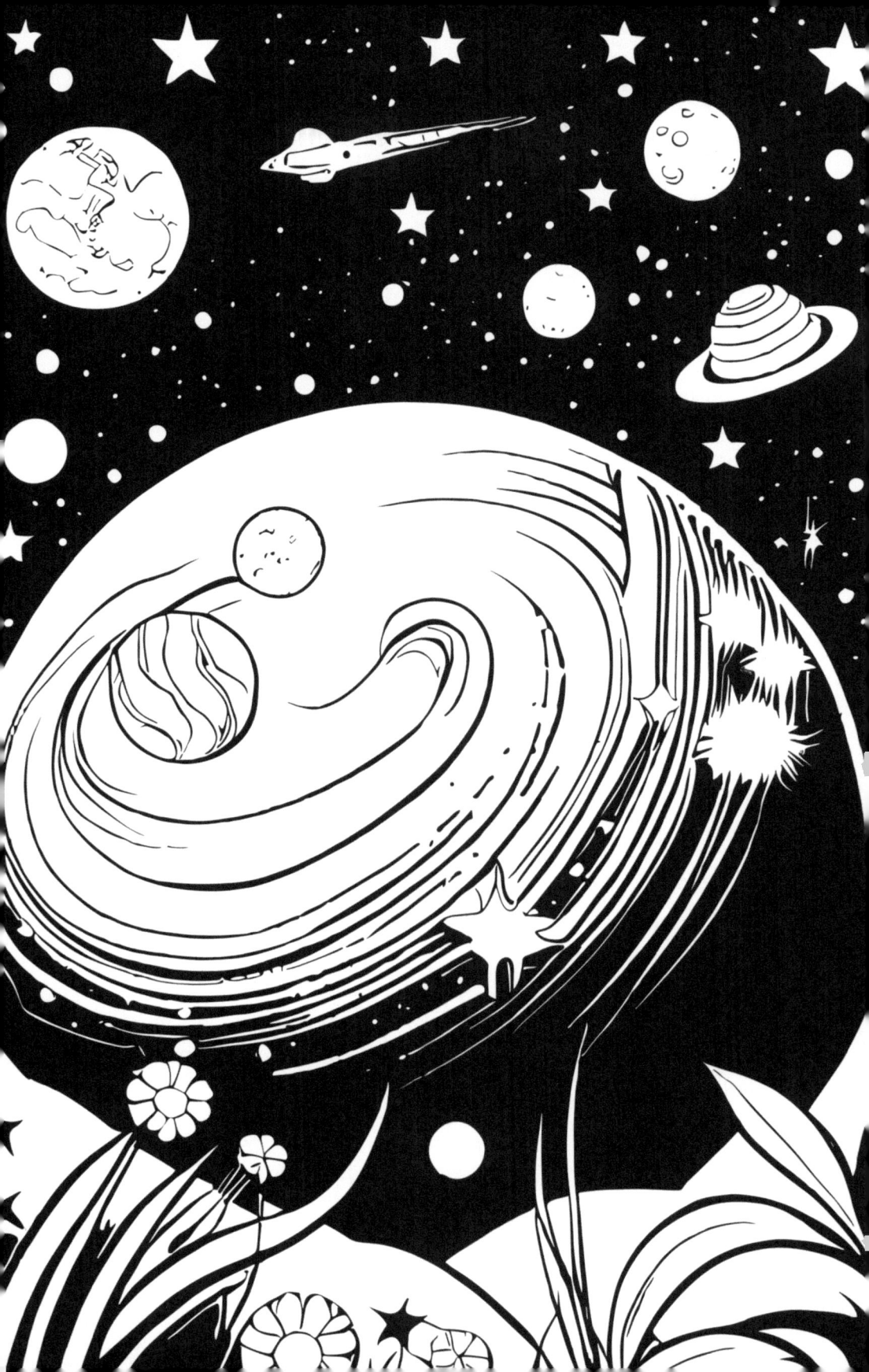

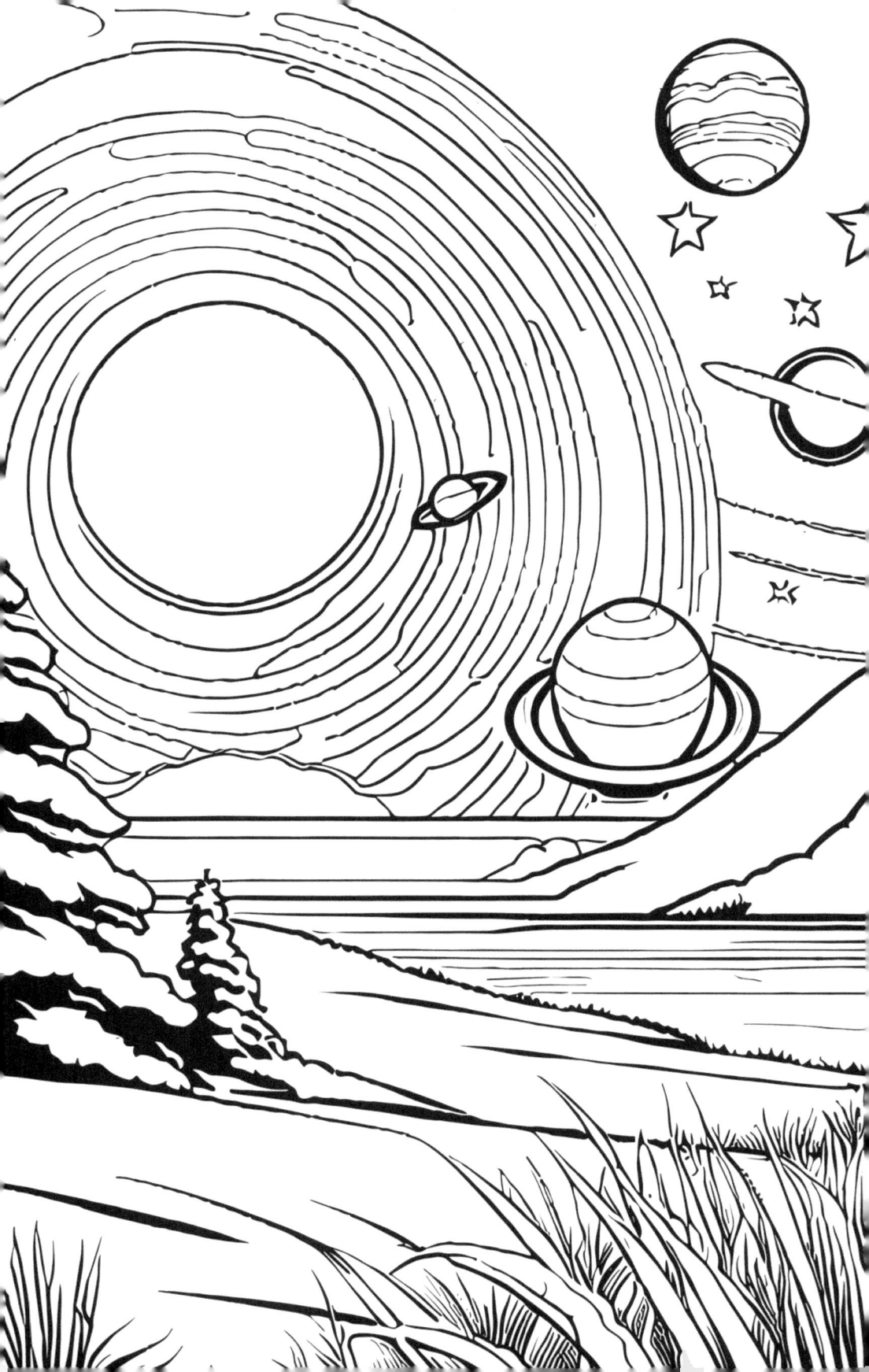

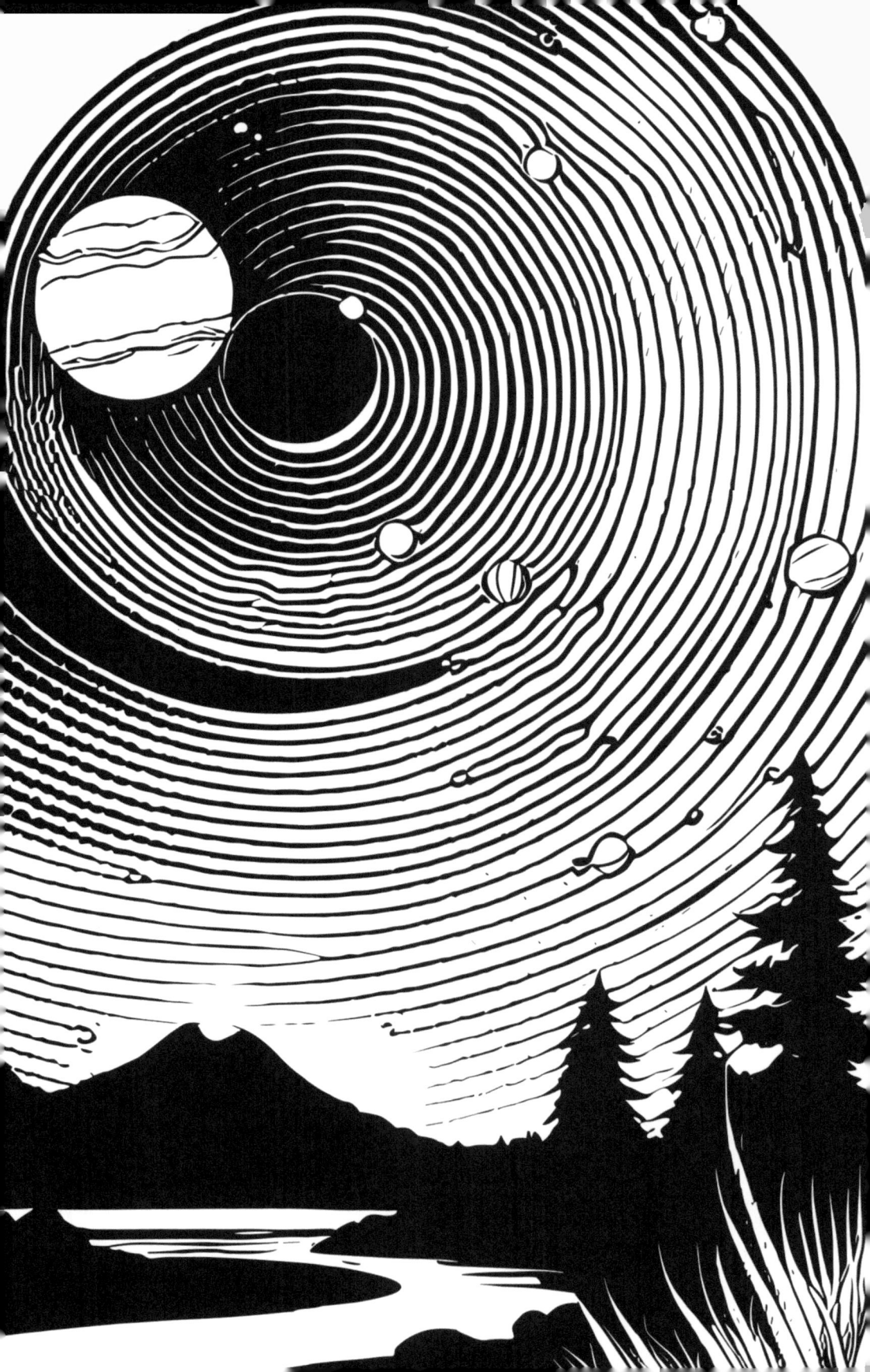

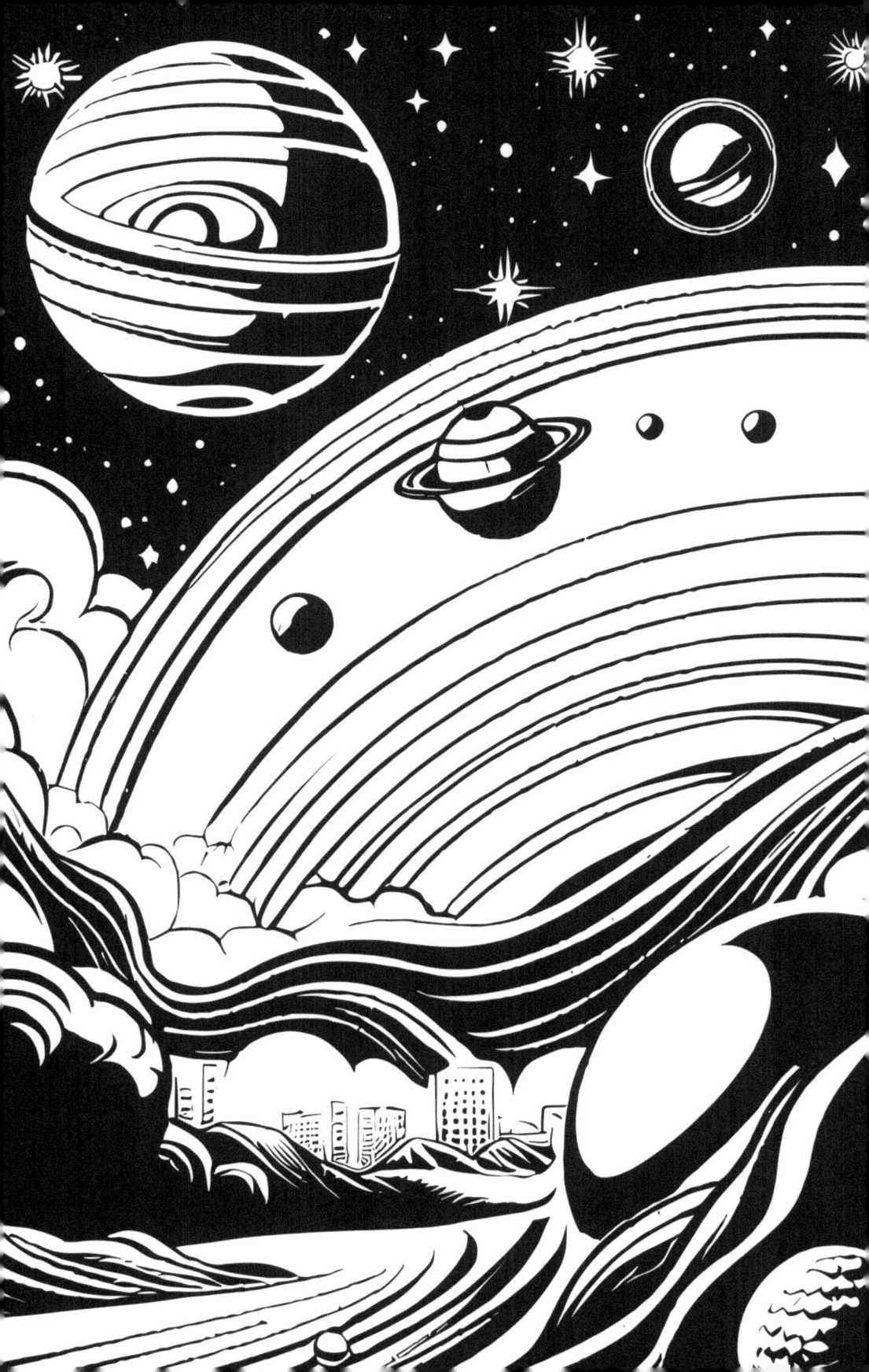

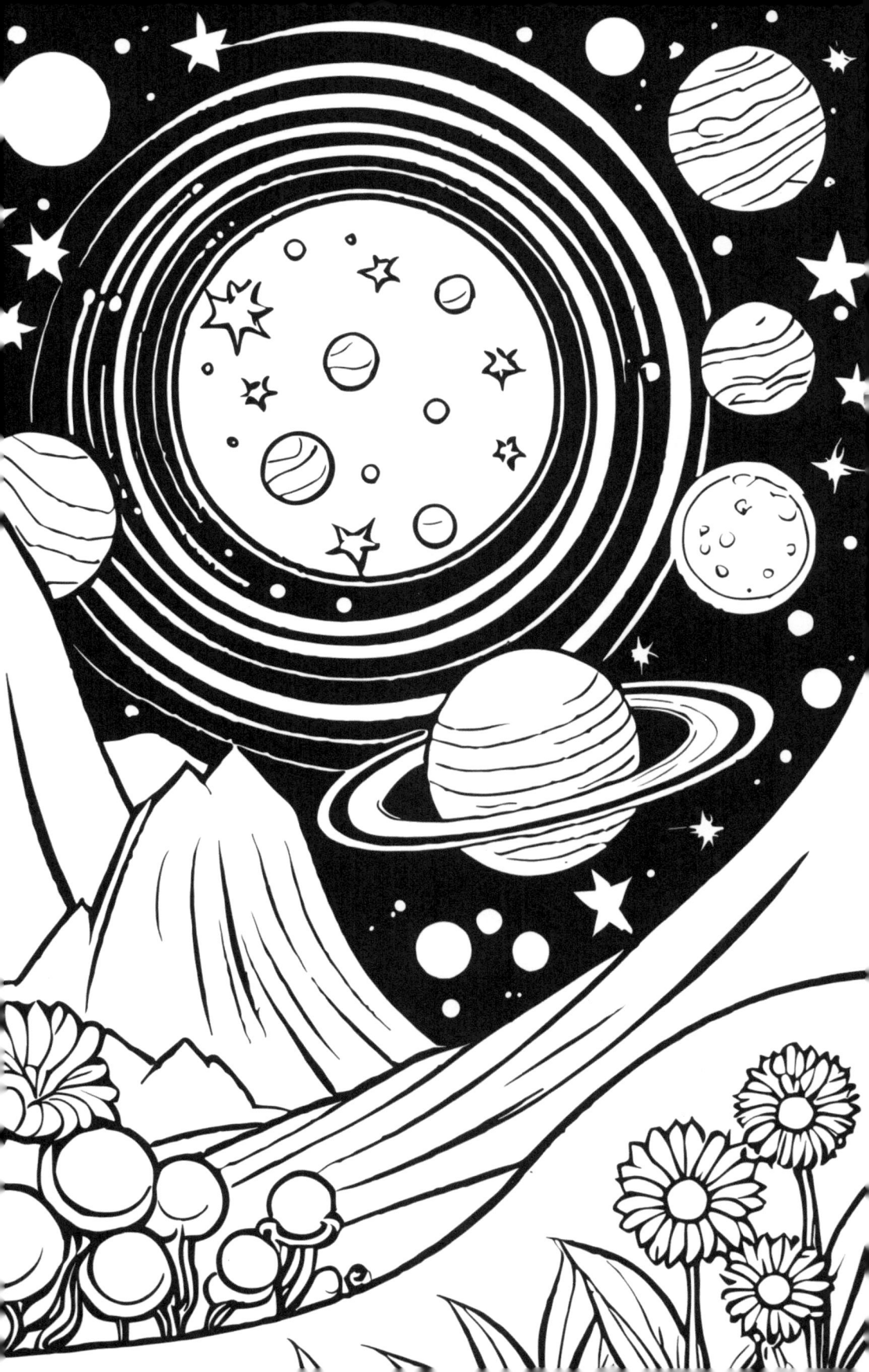

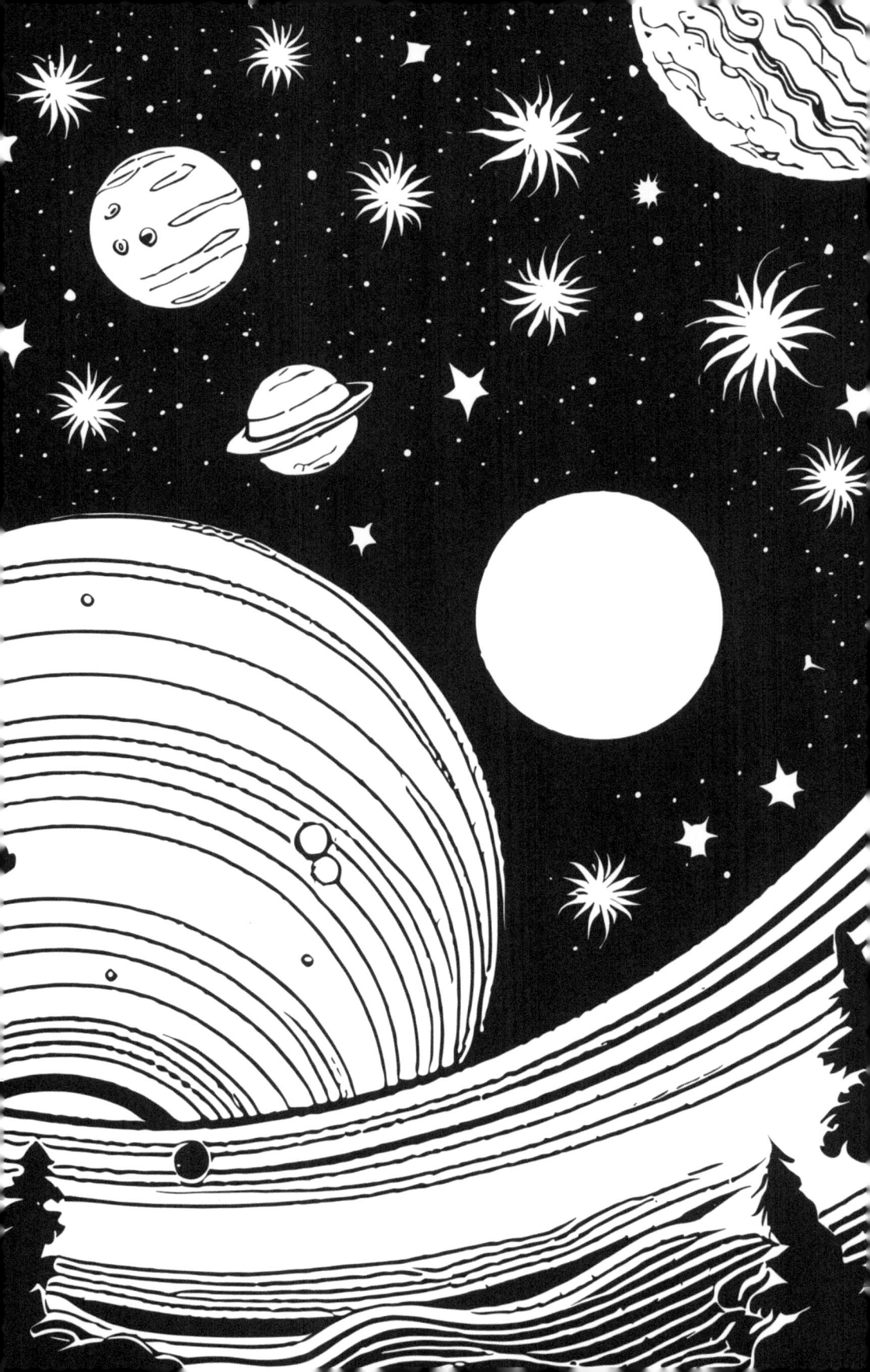

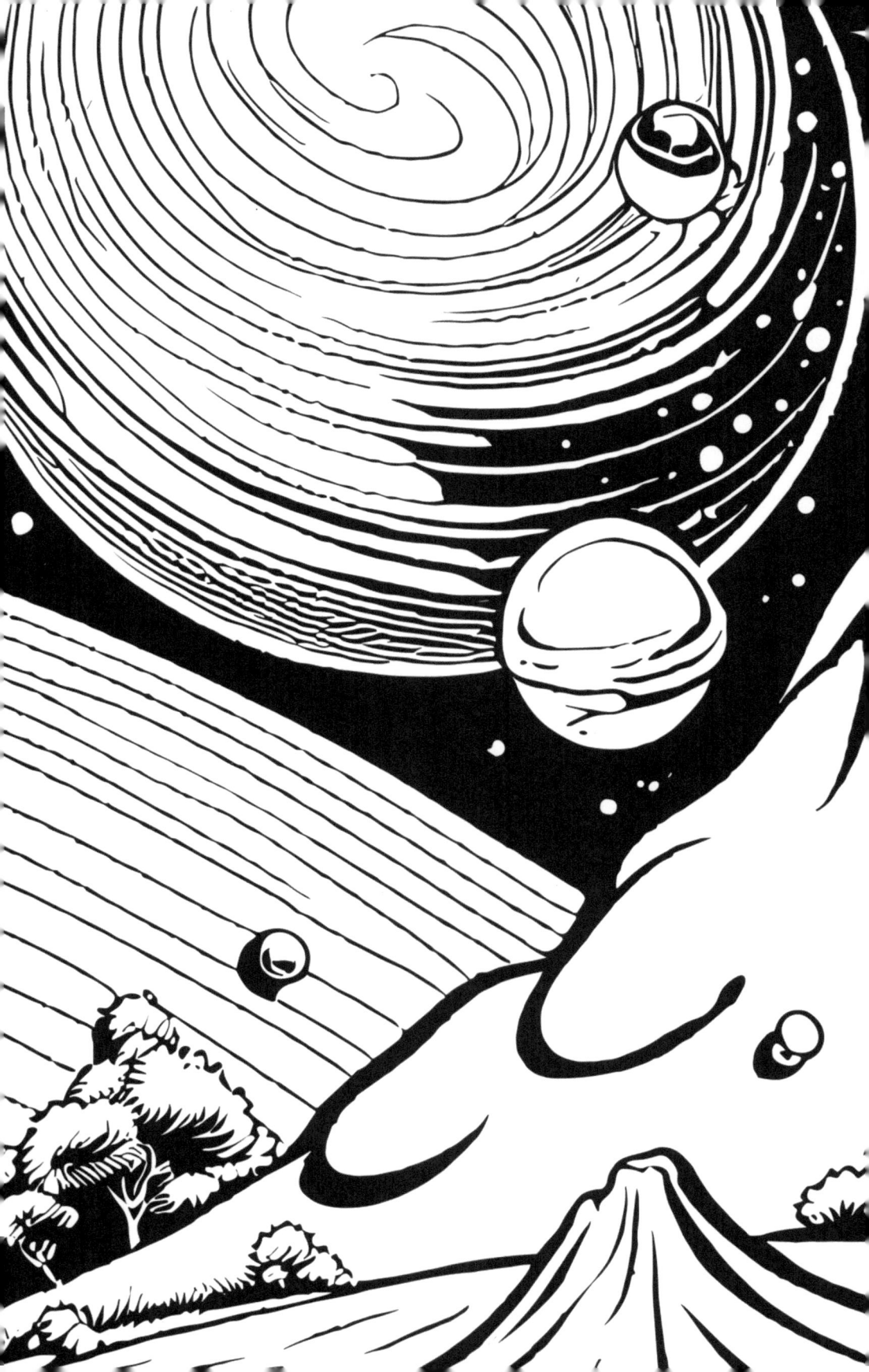

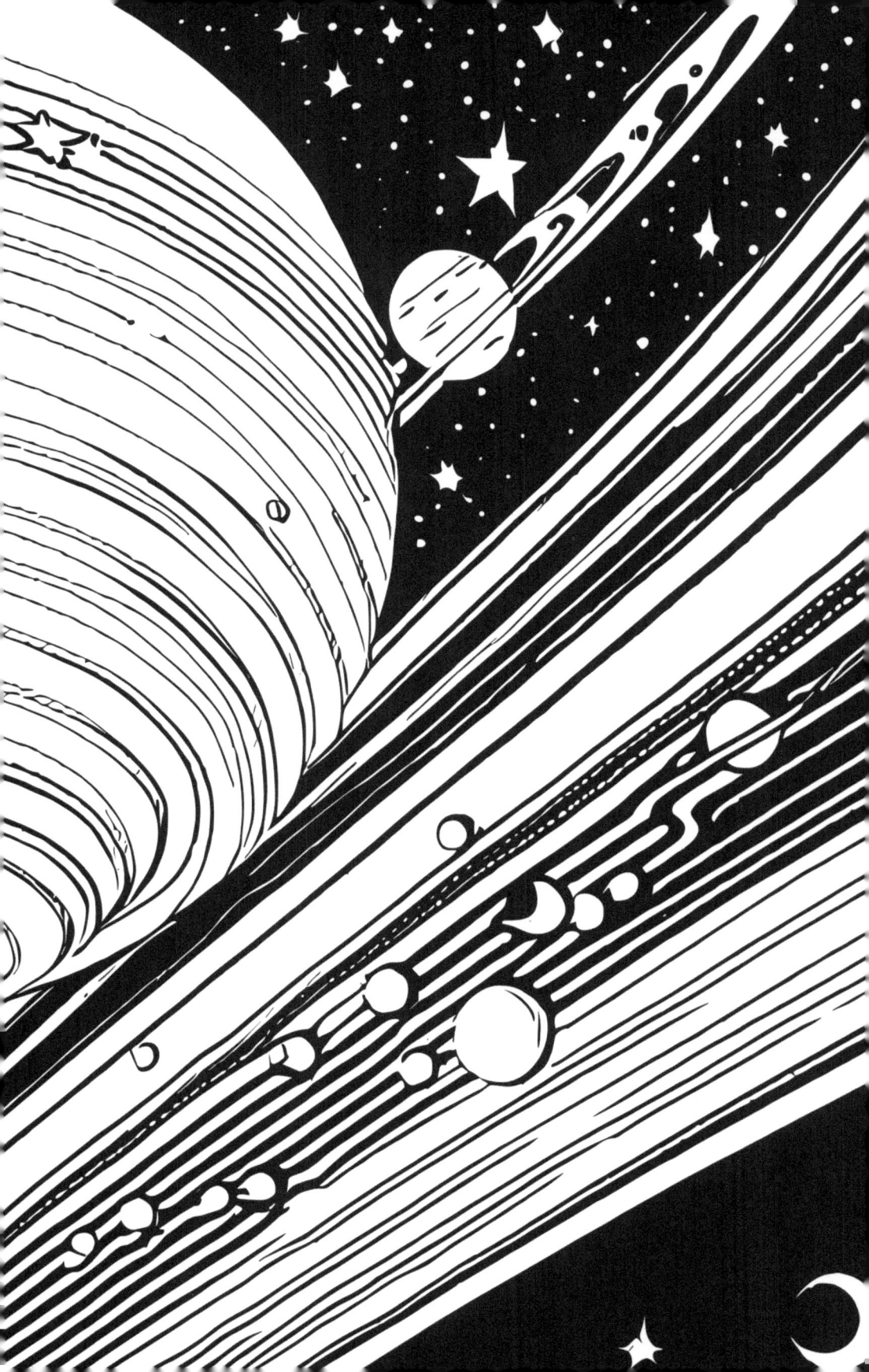

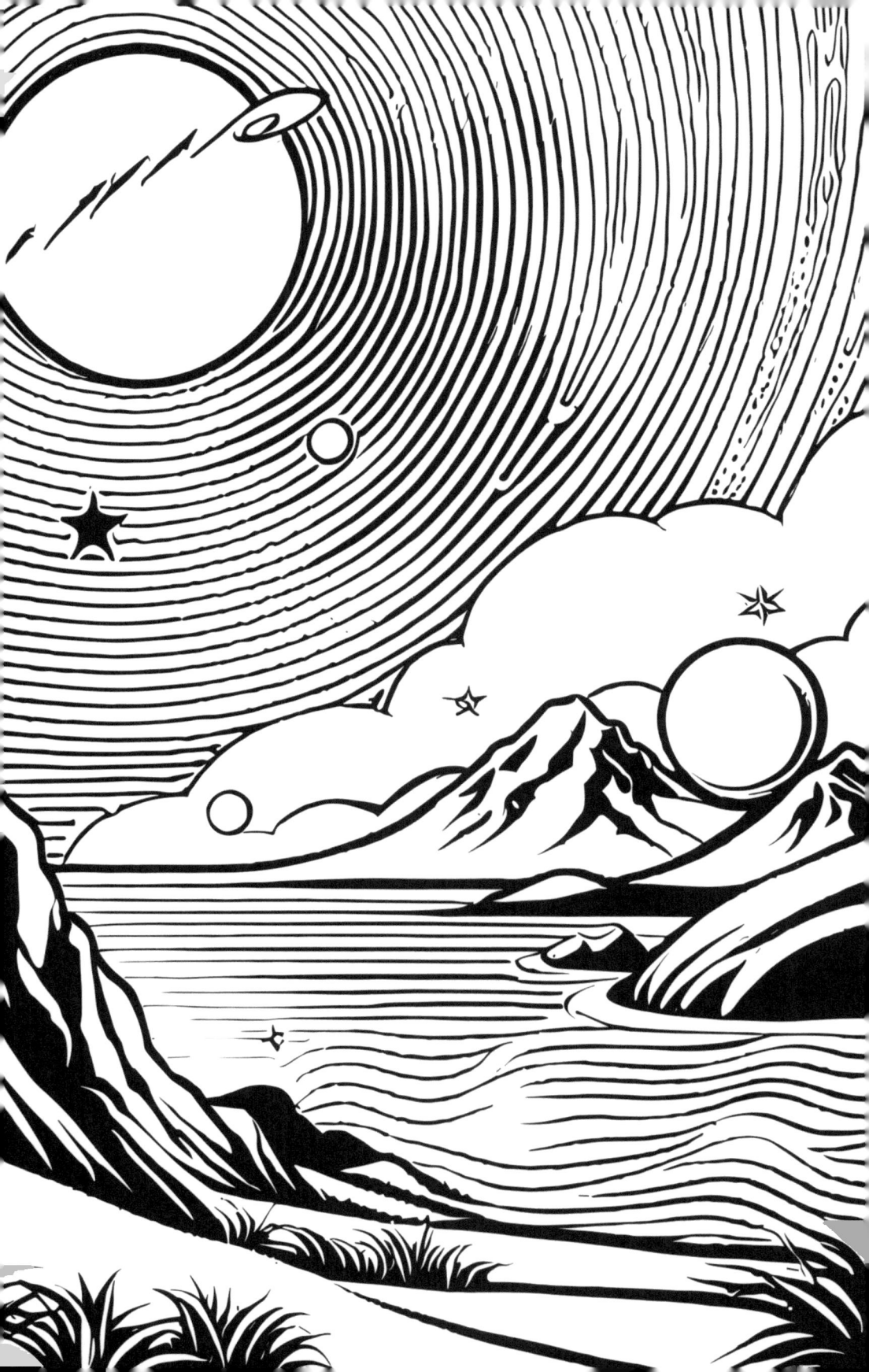

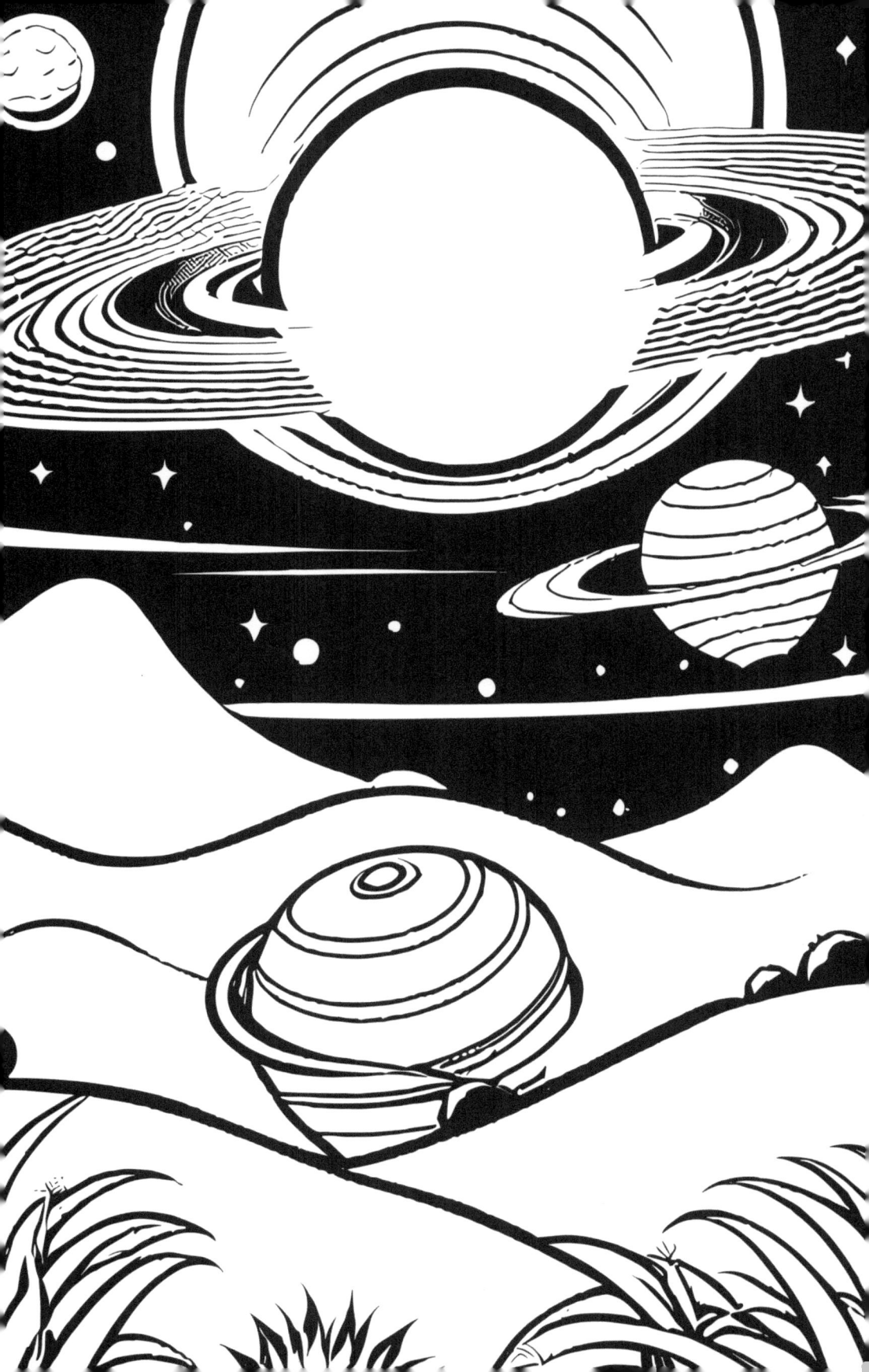

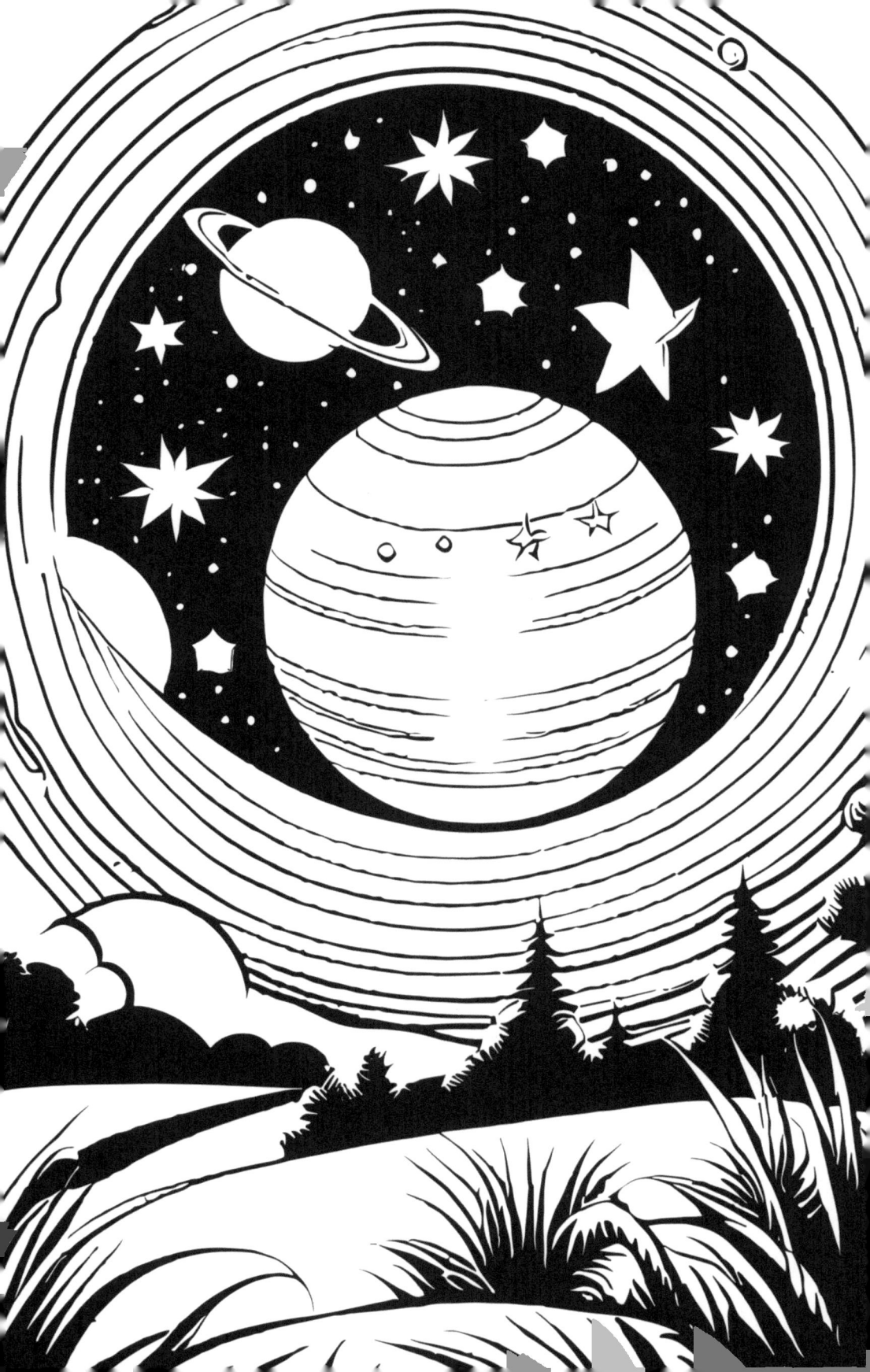

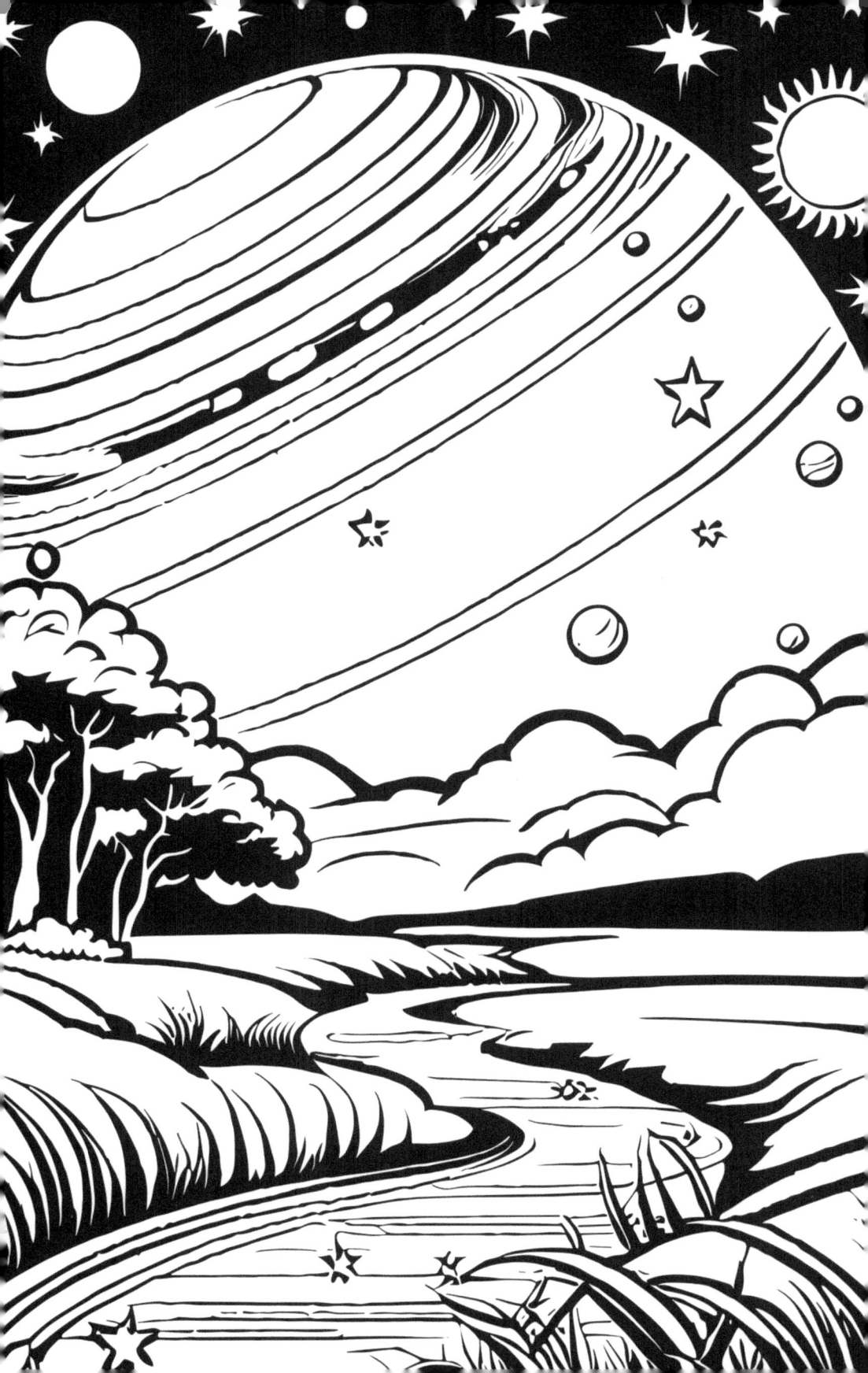

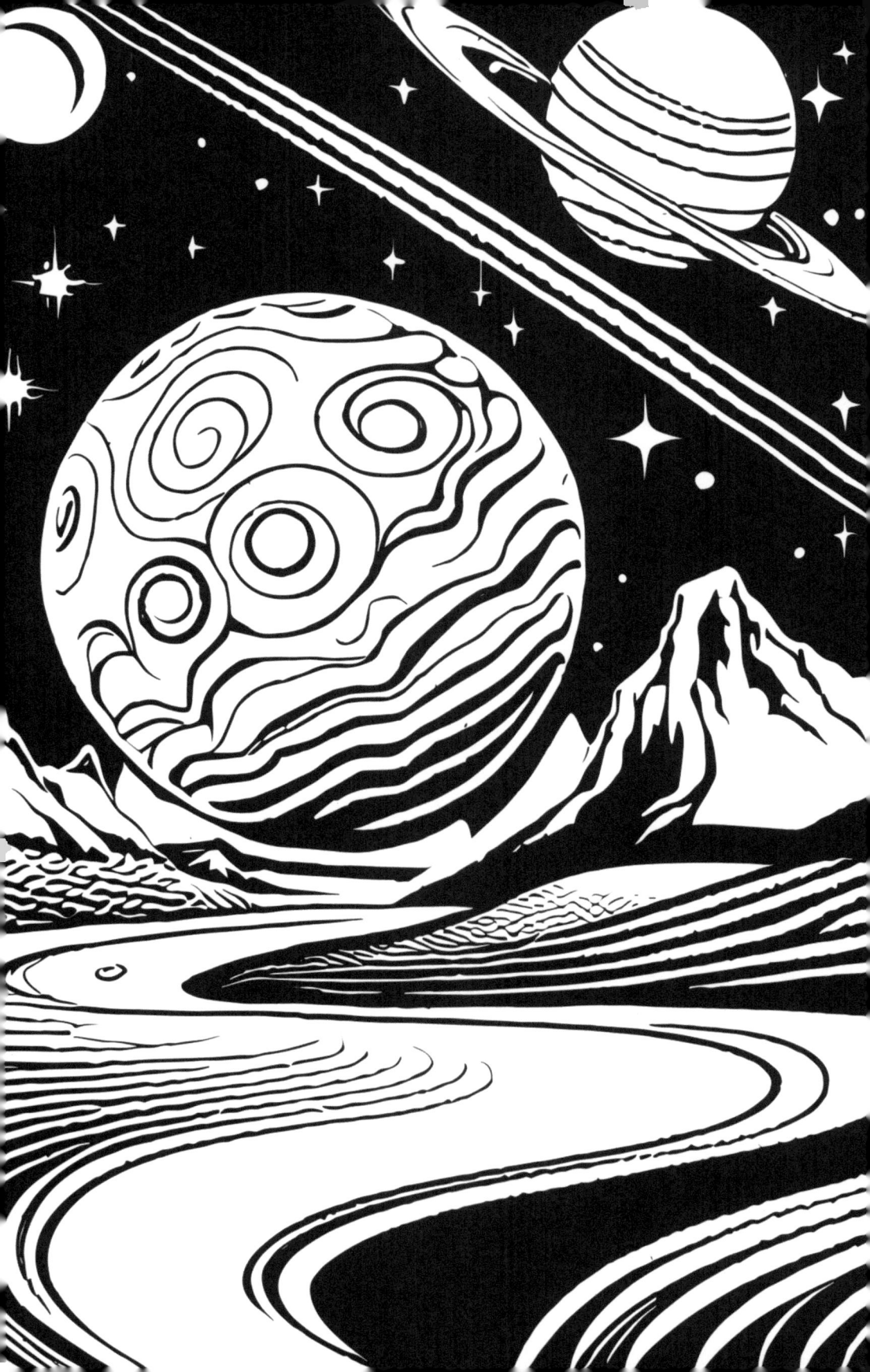

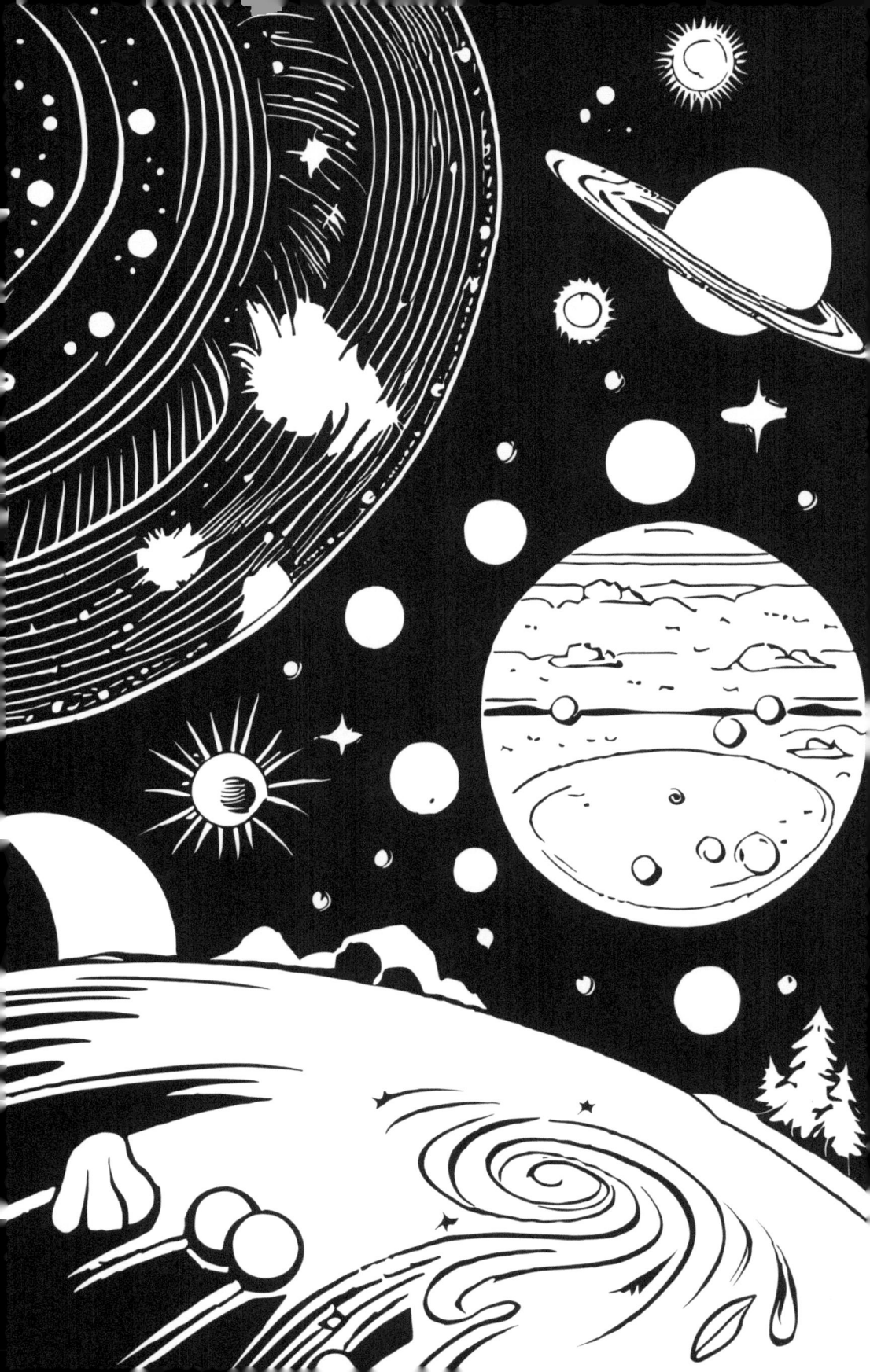

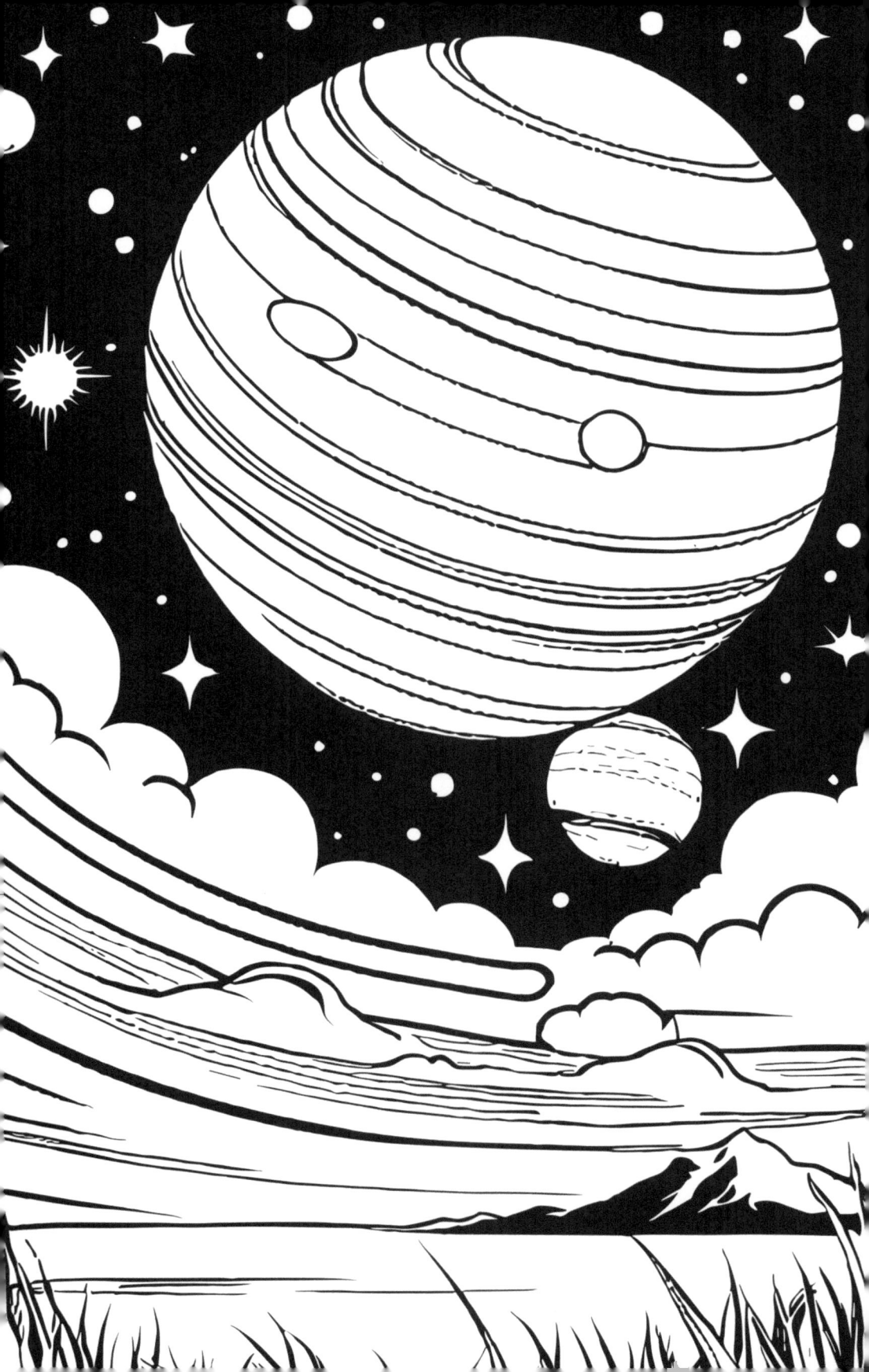

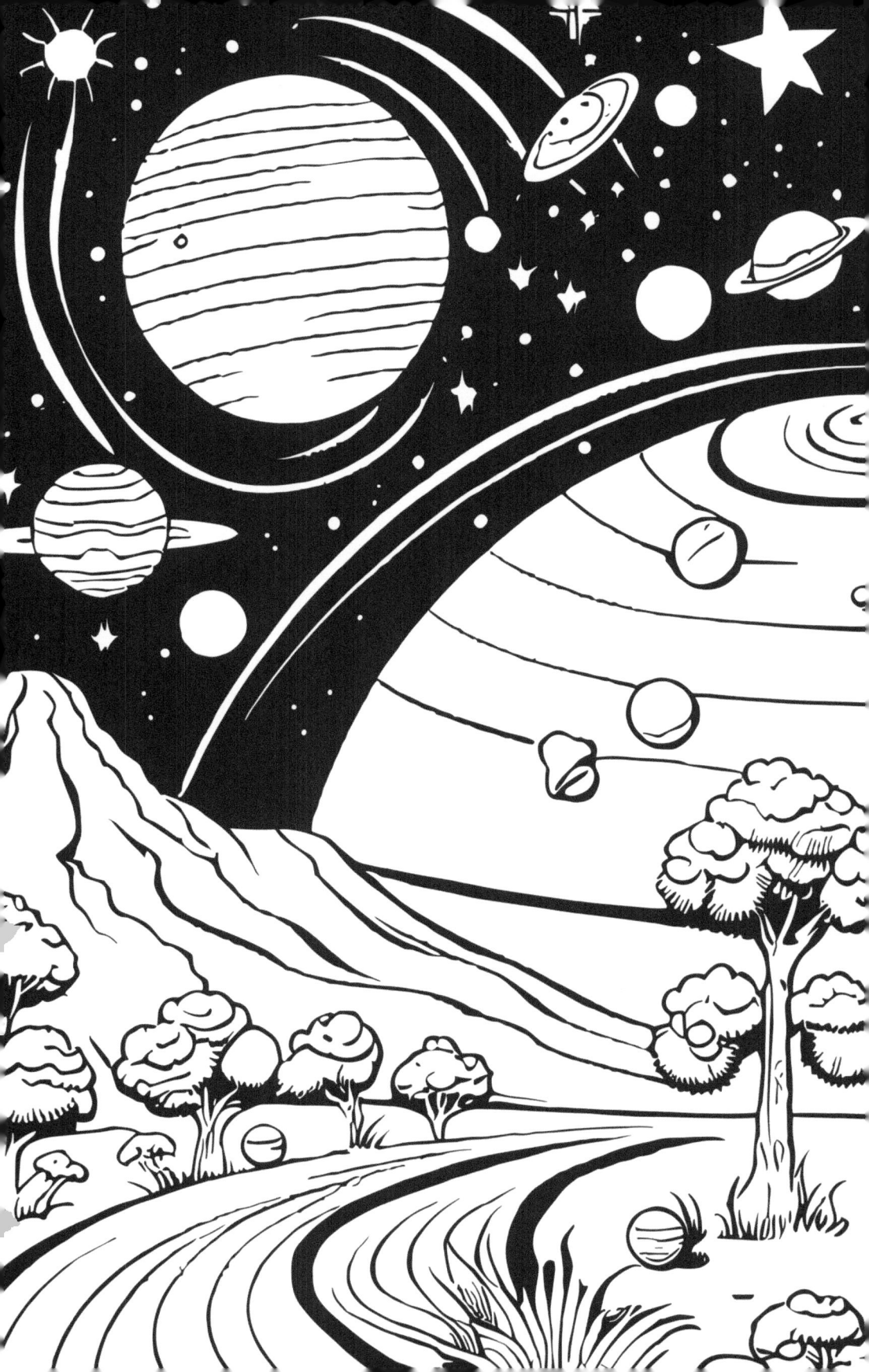

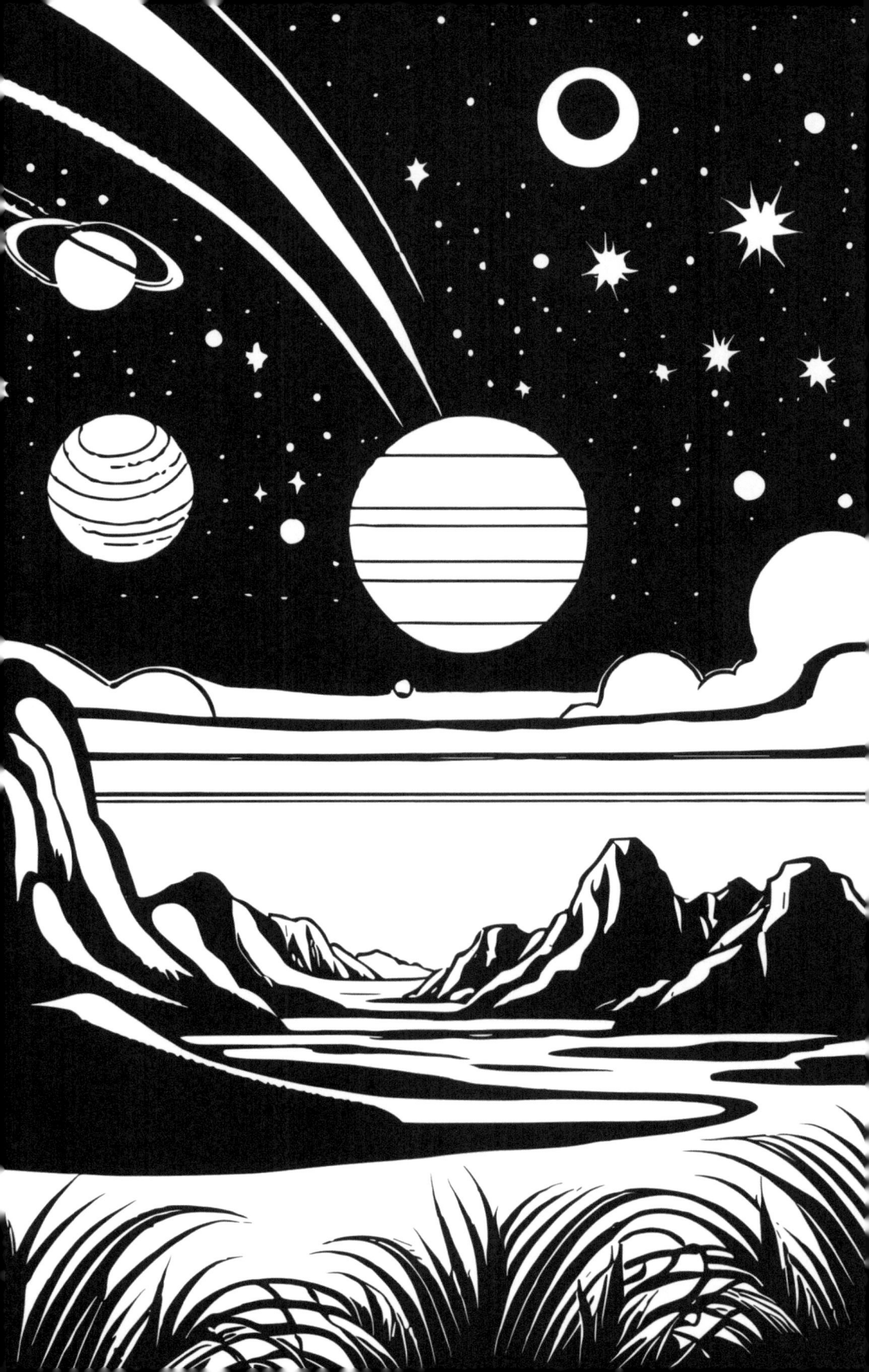

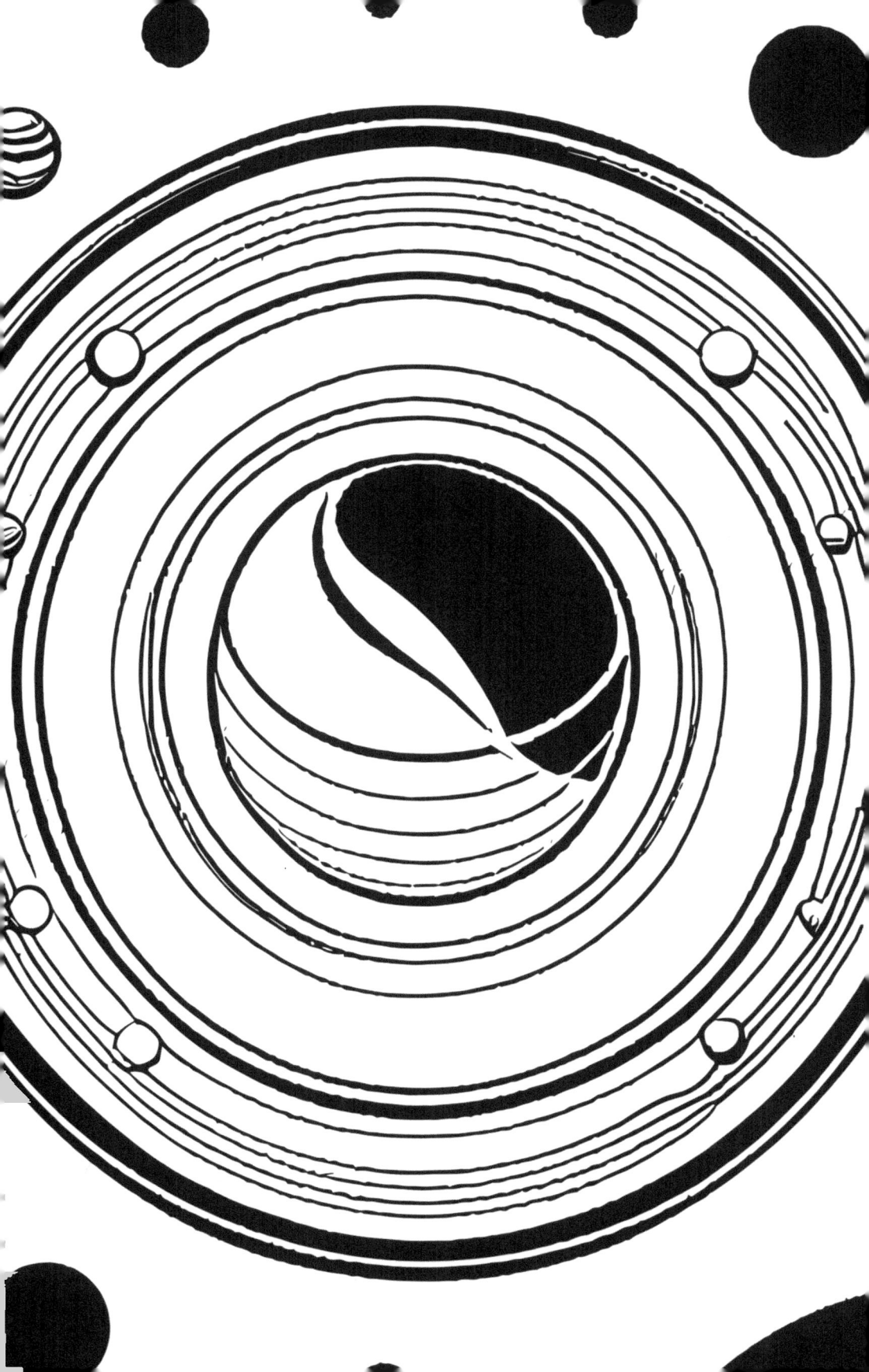

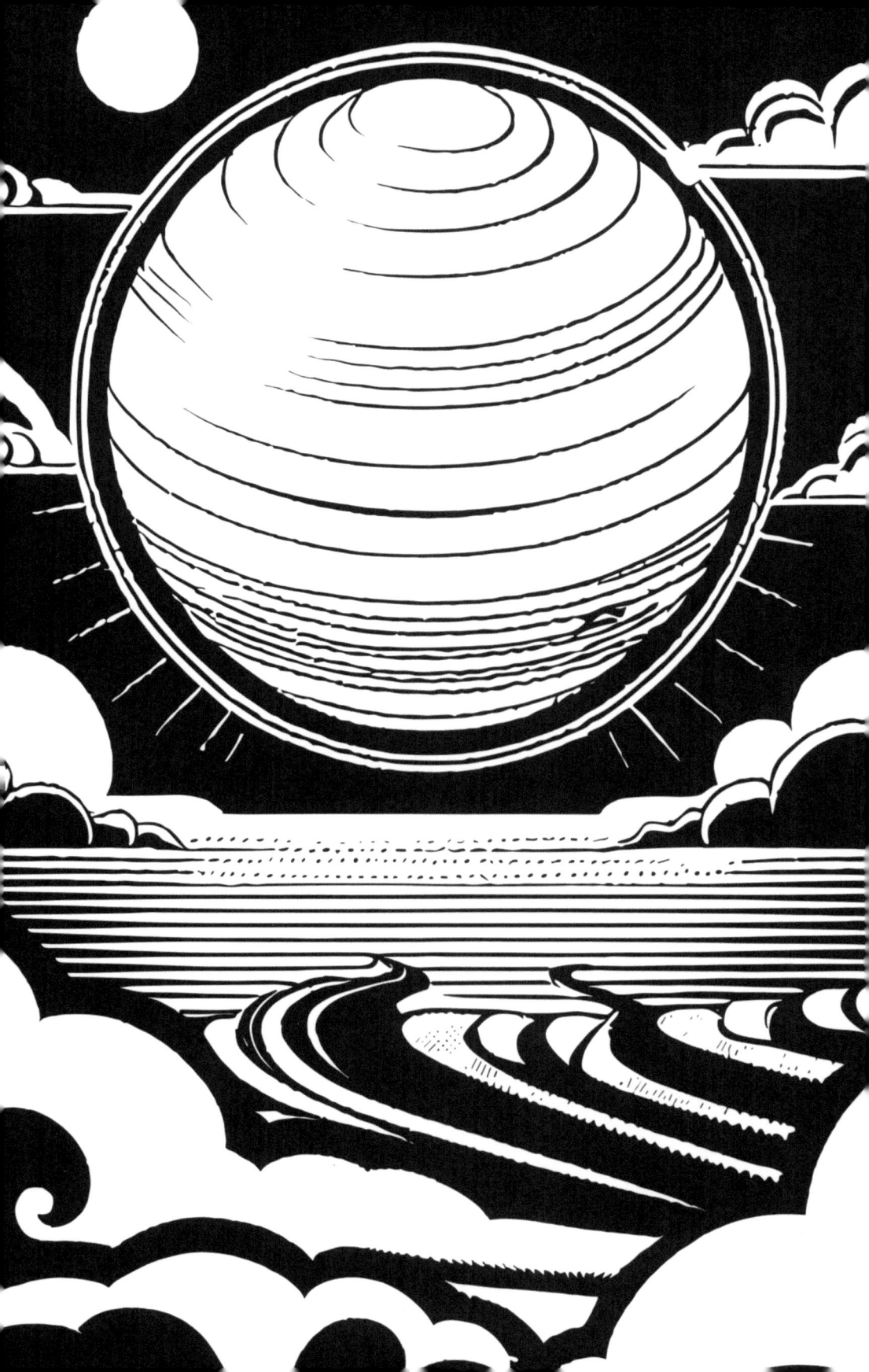

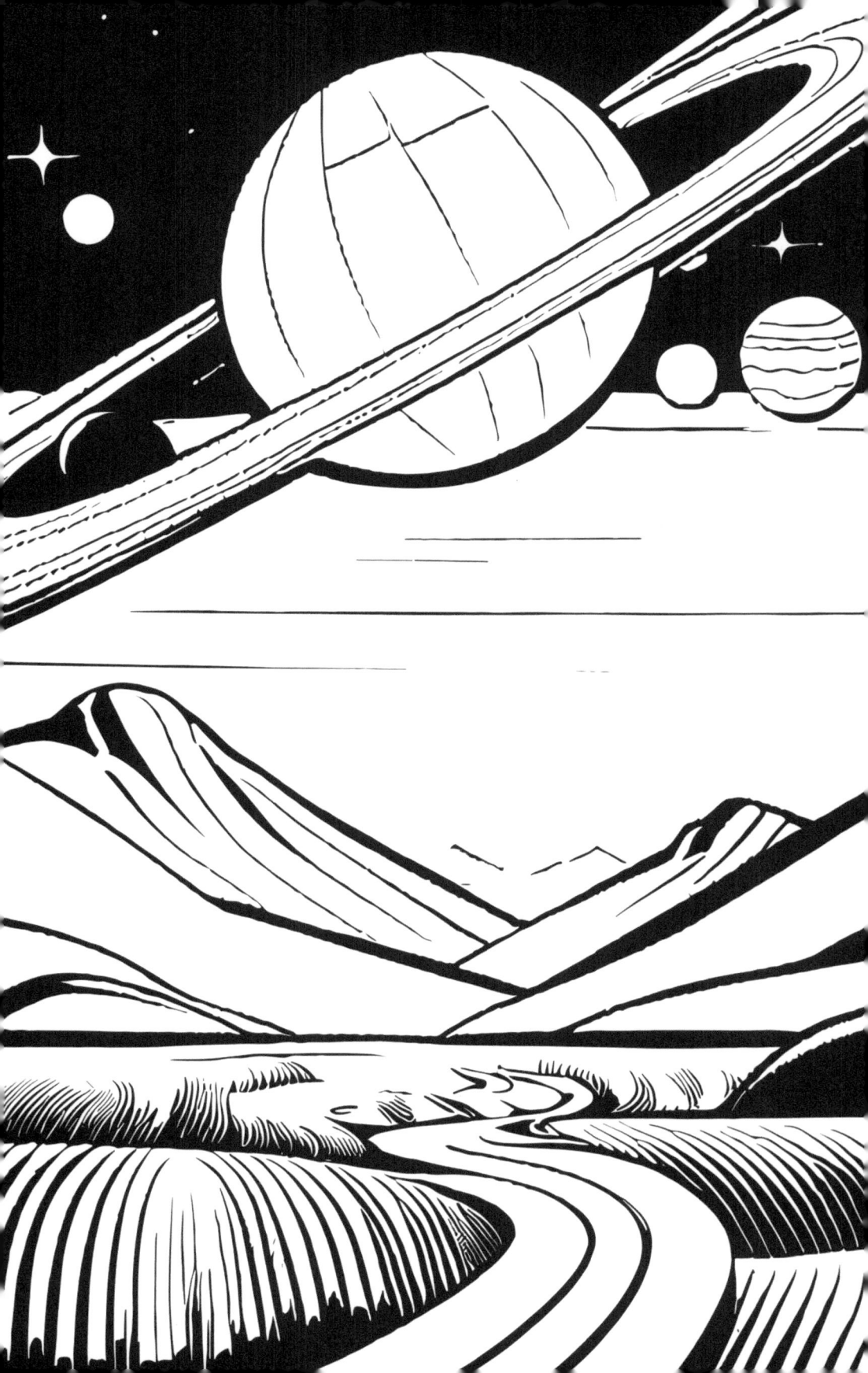

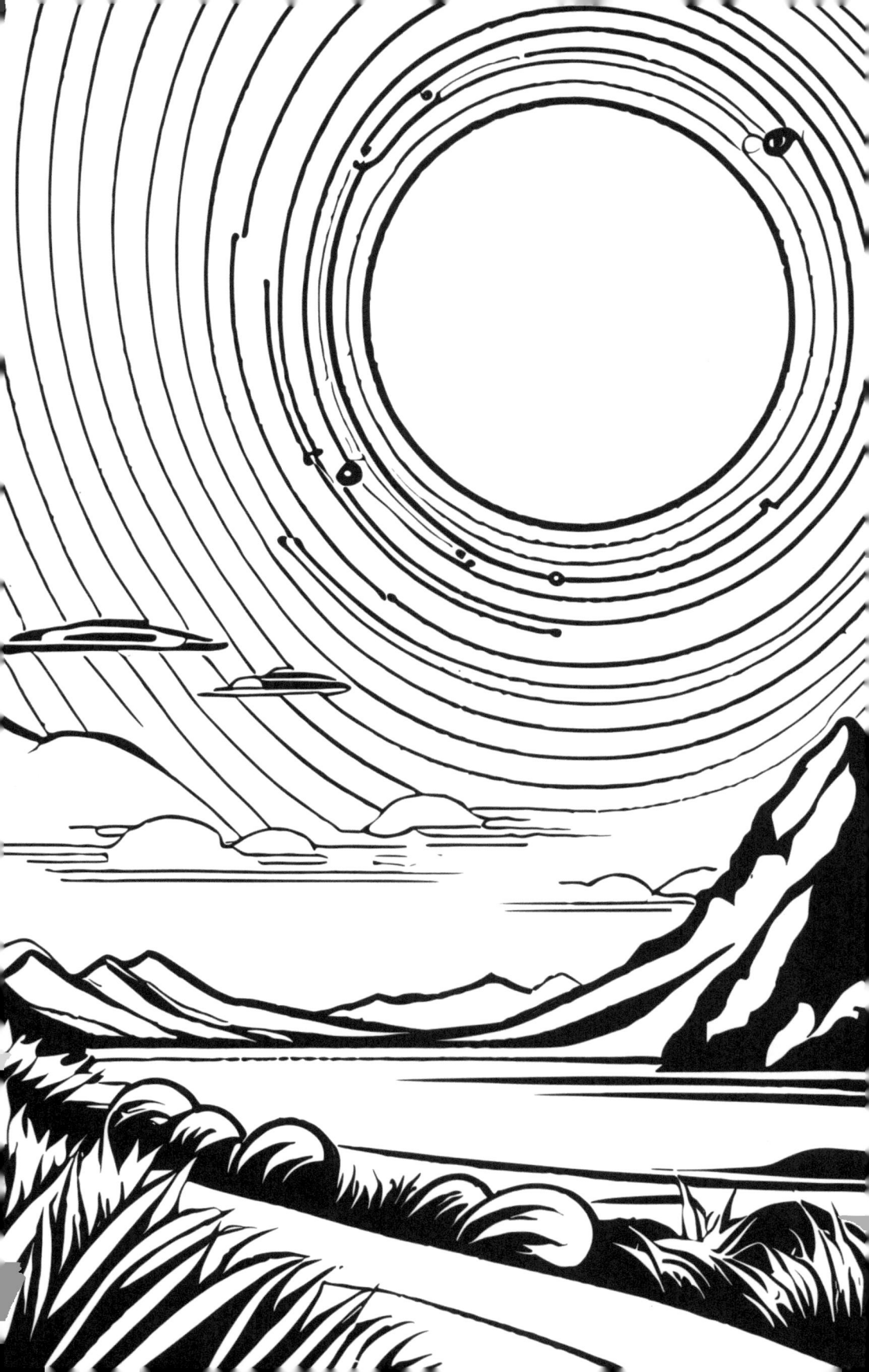

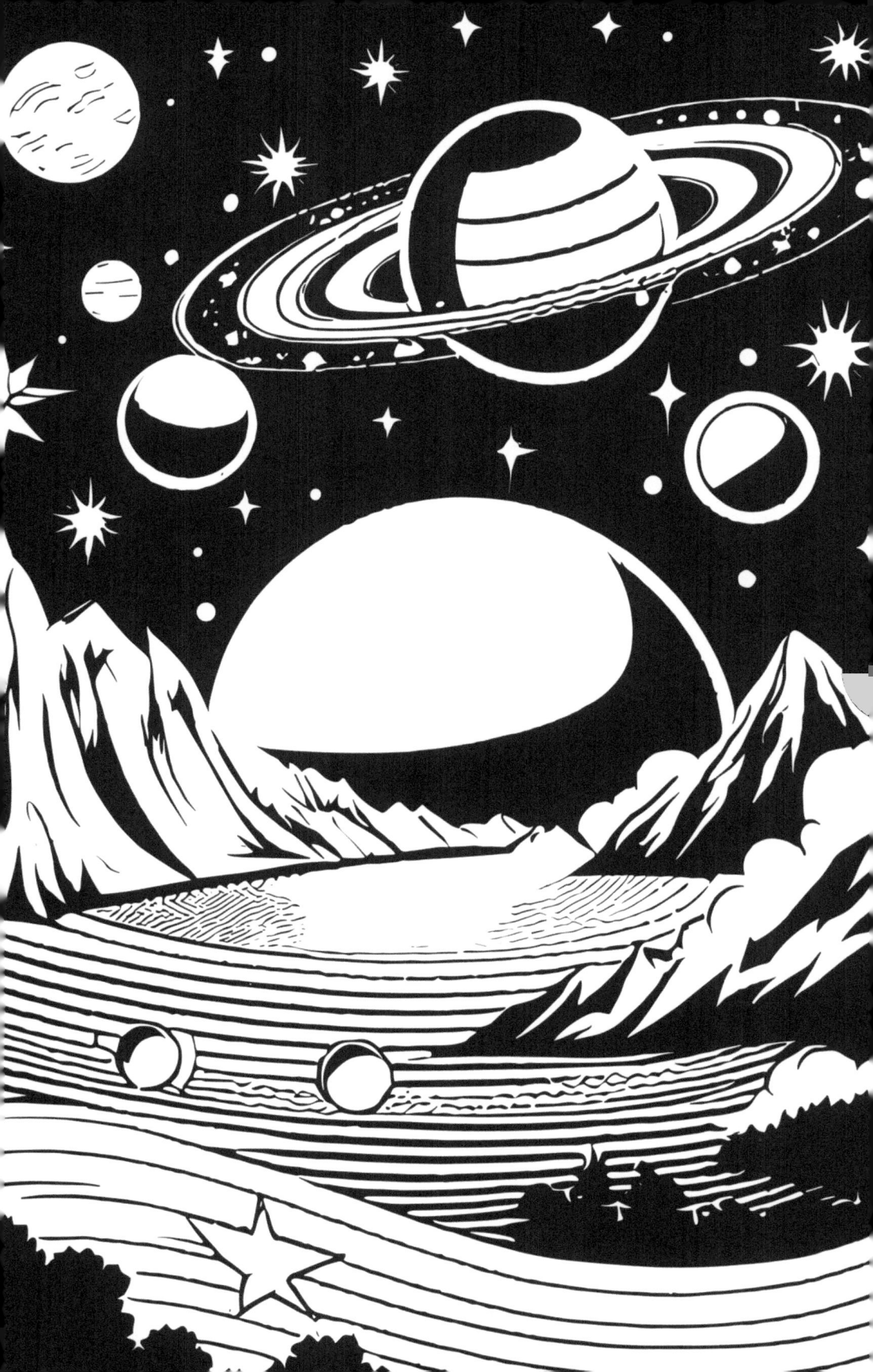

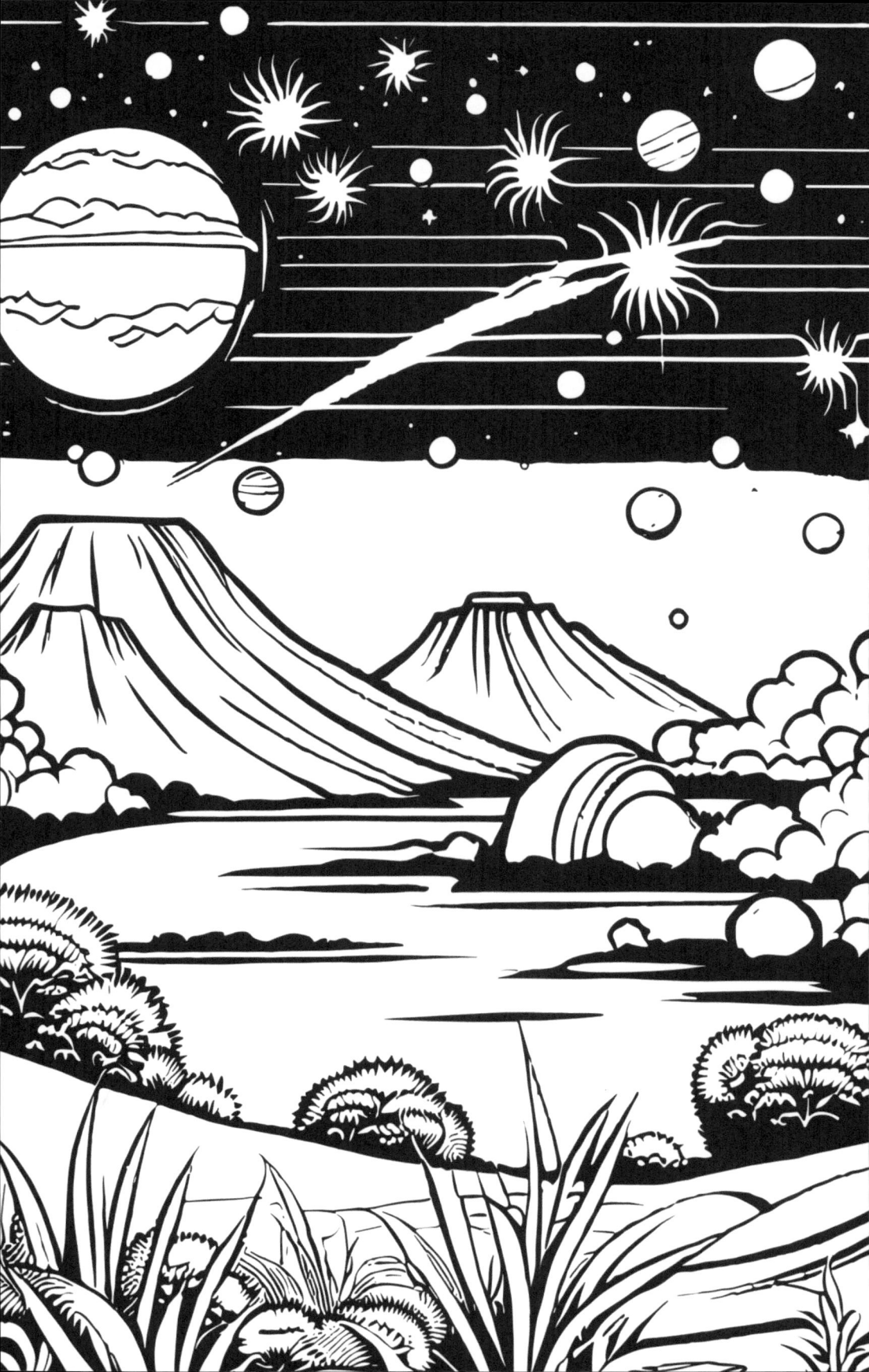

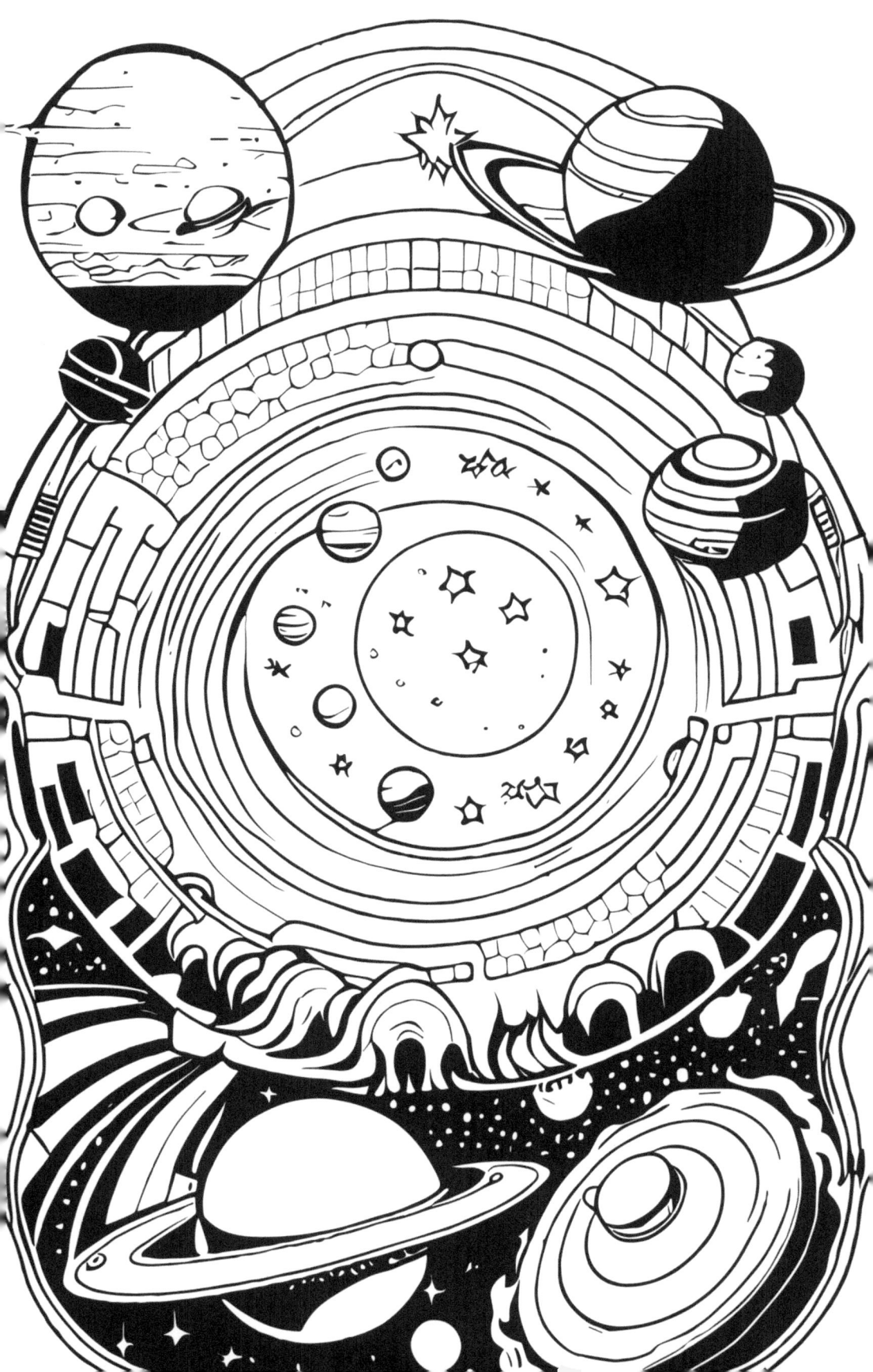

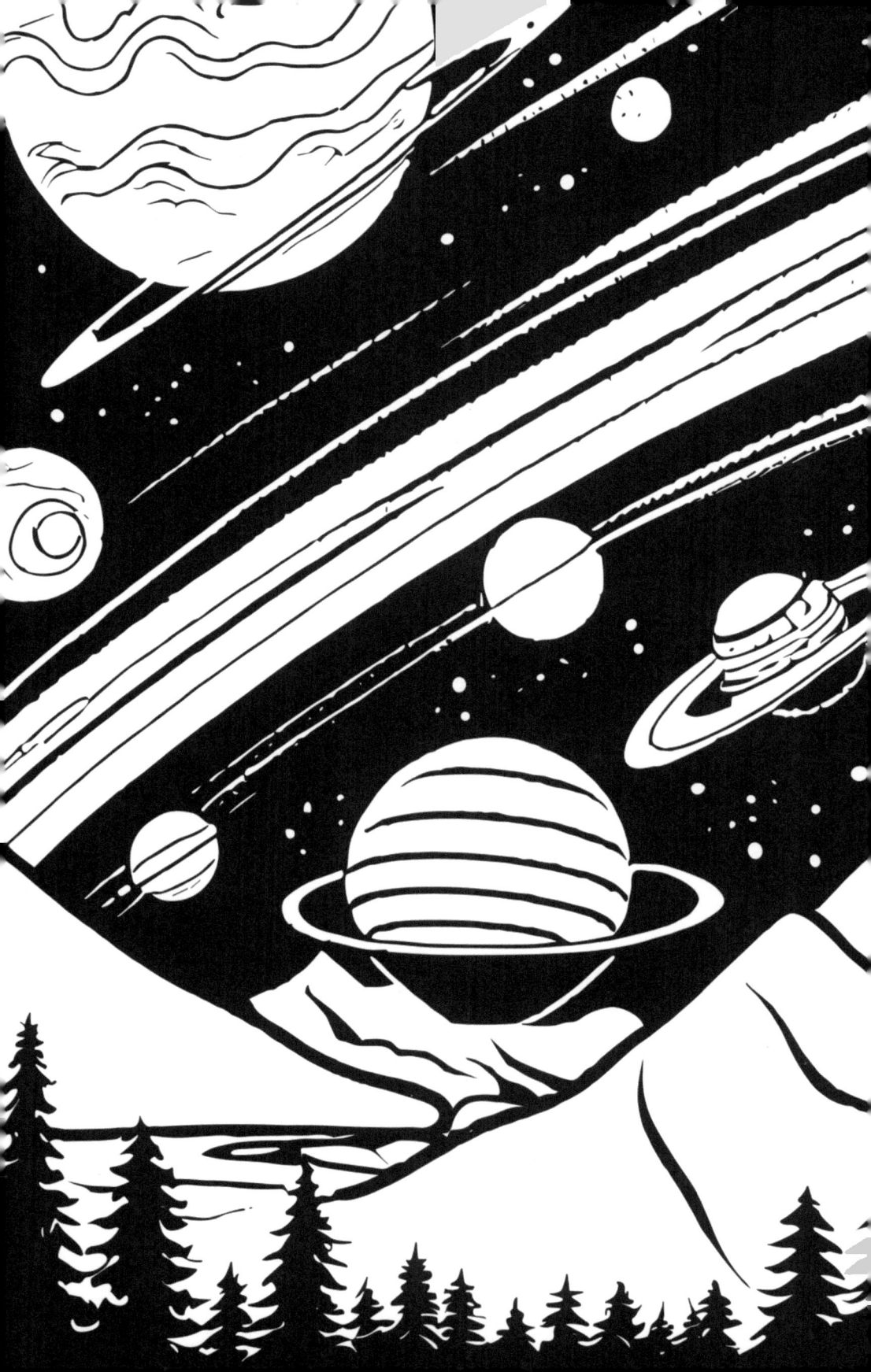

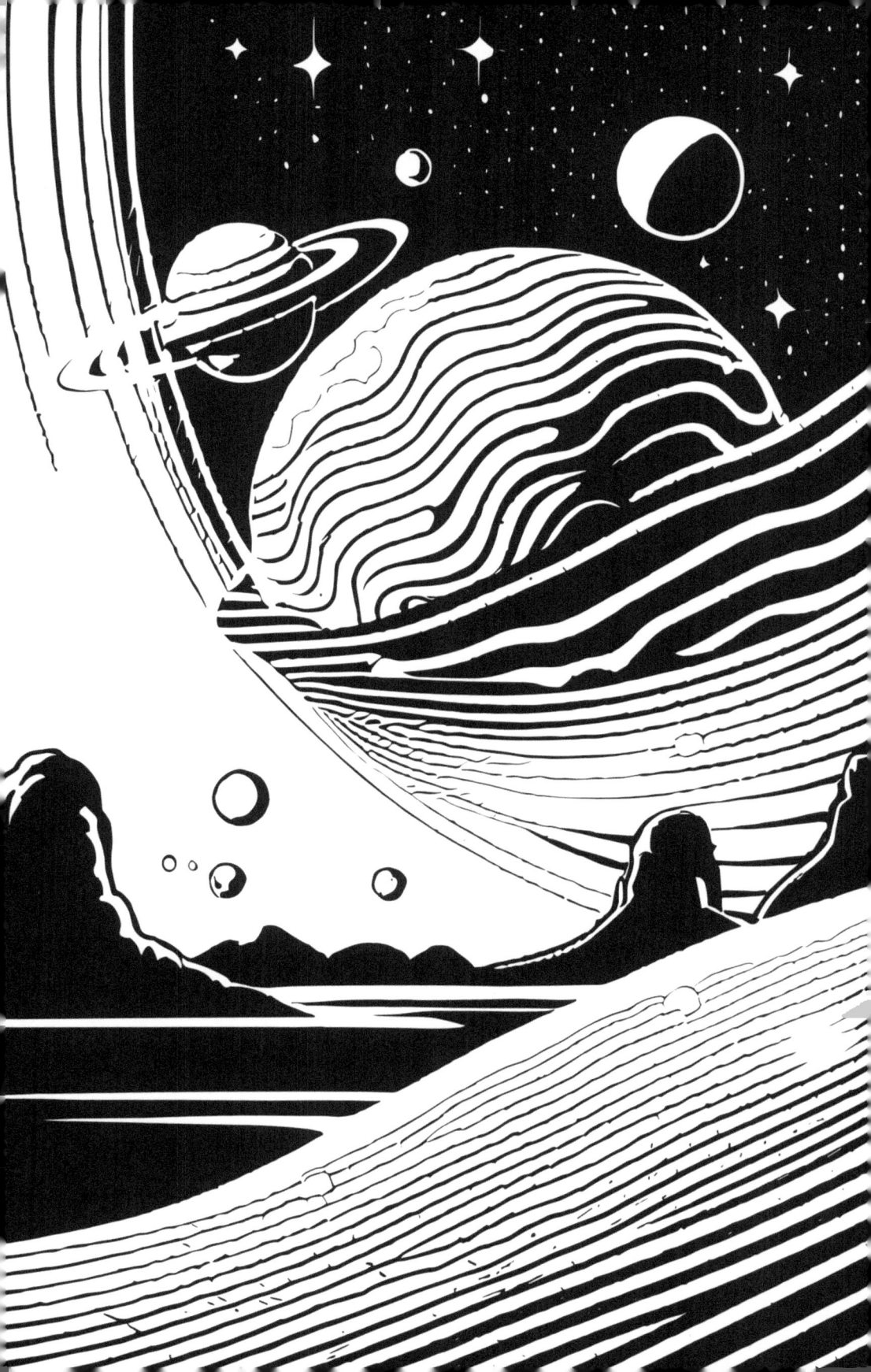

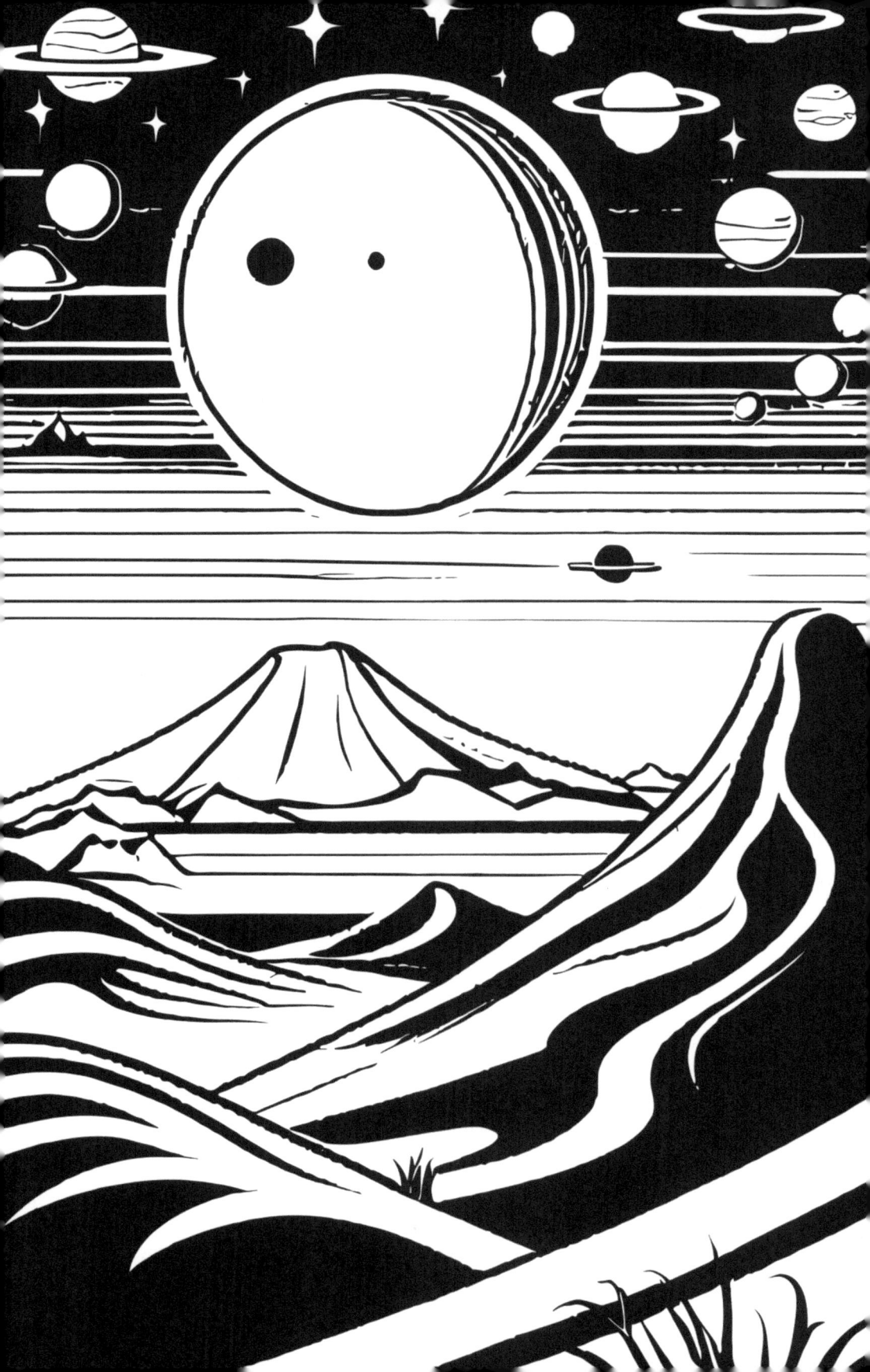

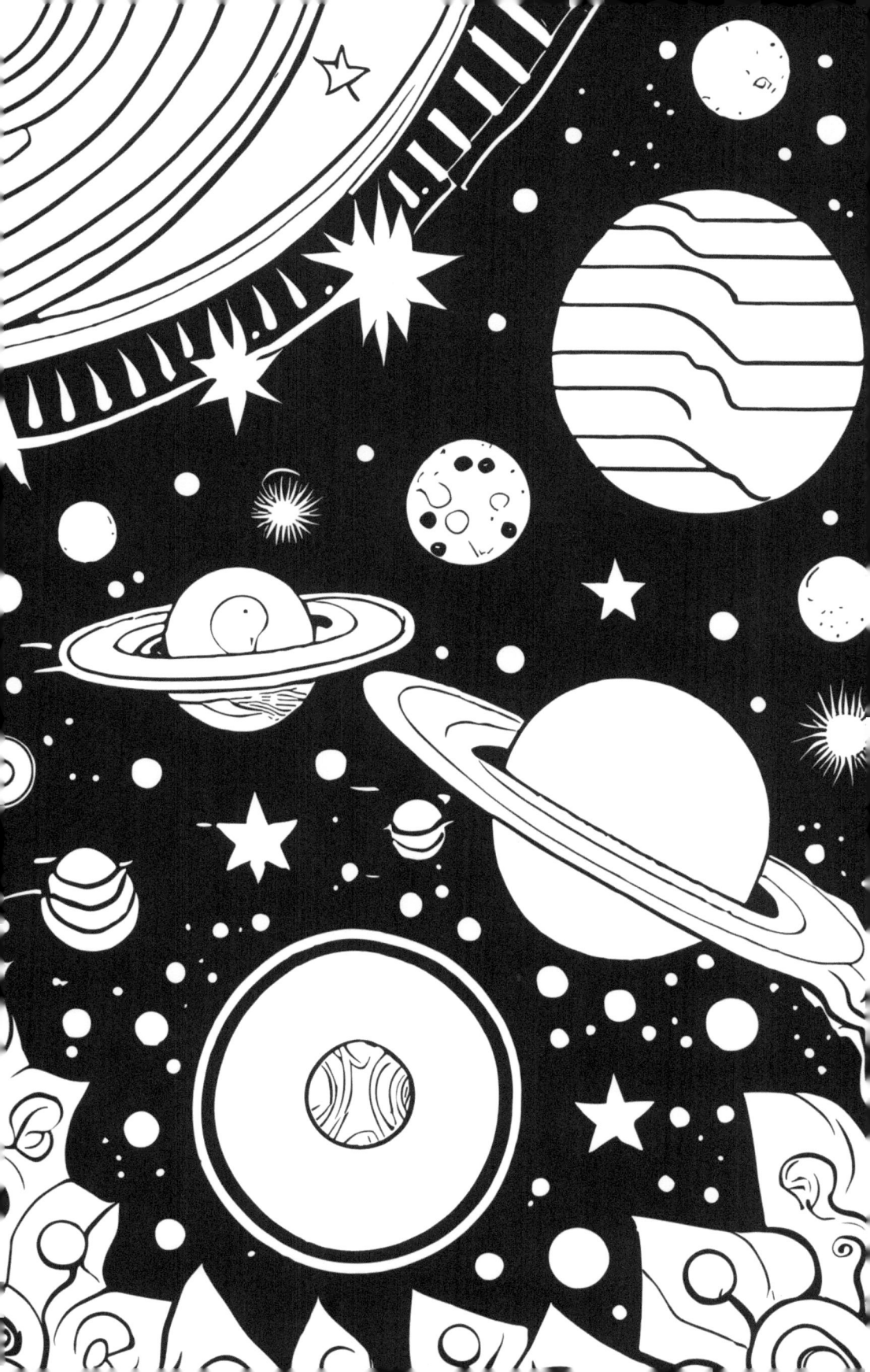

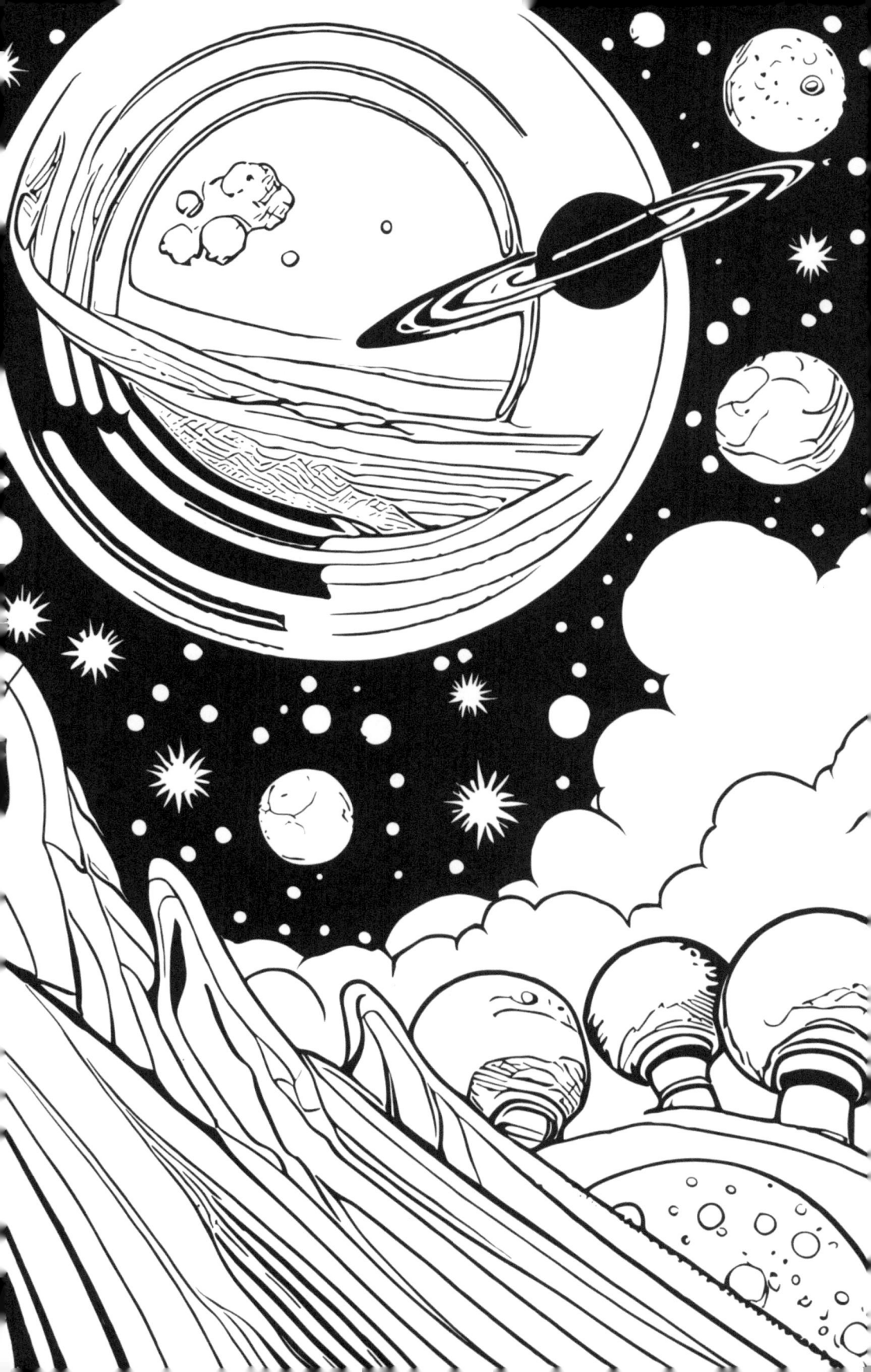

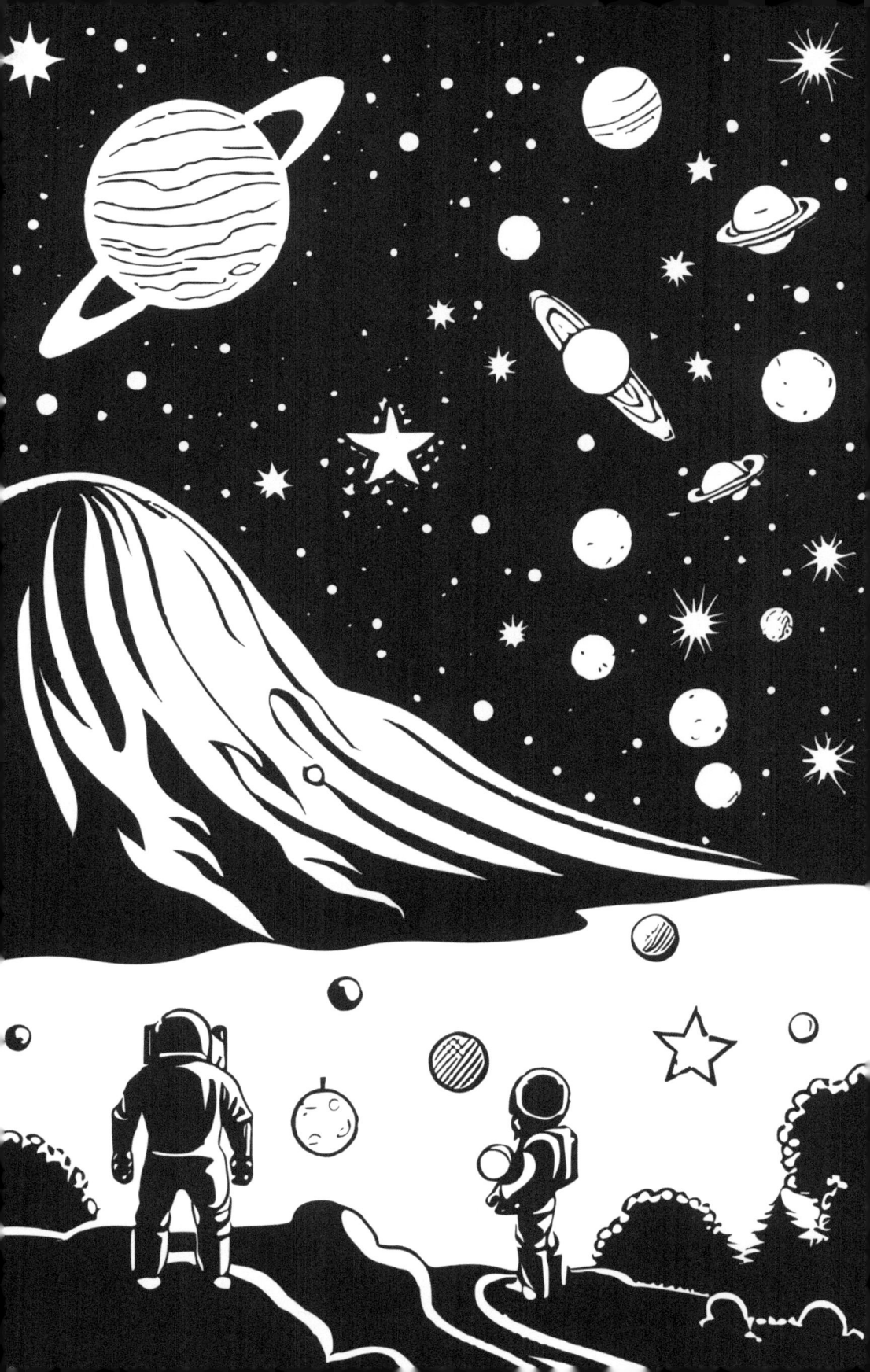

www.ingramcontent.com/pod-product-compliance
Lightning Source LLC
Chambersburg PA
CBHW040320010626
45792CB00024B/2072